.99p

C000042763

THE FIGHT
FOR YORKSHIRE

by

Michael Bradford

HUTTON PRESS

1988

Published by the Hutton Press Ltd.
130 Canada Drive, Cherry Burton, Beverley
East Yorkshire HU17 7SB

Printed and Bound by

Clifford Ward & Co. (Bridlington) Ltd.
55 West Street, Bridlington, East Yorkshire
YO15 3DZ

ISBN 0 907033 66 0

CONTENTS

FOREWORD

What happened to Yorkshire in 1974? Changes were introduced which Parliament said were for local government. But to many ordinary people they seemed like an assault on themselves — on the settled geography of centuries and on their own identity. Their reactions, at a historic moment of transition, should not go unrecorded, both for their own sake, and in order that any lessons may be learned.

But another motive drives this — the hope that, in spite of everything, people will not cease to remember what and where Yorkshire is. With this in view, though elsewhere administrative maps are the only kind now available, the County of York is shown on the maps herein, its boundaries with unbroken lines.

Michael Bradford
Headingley
April 1988

ACKNOWLEDGEMENTS

The following pages could not have been written without help from many people whom I wish to thank here. I am grateful to the many authors and publishers mentioned in the text for allowing the use of the material concerned. Passages from Department of the Environment Circulars, the 1972 Local Government Act, and the Report of the Royal Commission on Local Government in England, 1966-69 ("The Maud Report") are reproduced with the permission of the Controller of Her Majesty's Stationery Office; and I must mention the helpfulness of officers of the DoE itself in providing records of the committee stages of the local government Bill. Reference Librarians in Bristol, Oxford and Warrington gave access to records concerning Berkshire, Lancashire, Gloucestershire and Somerset; and I received information on Rutland from Mr. R. Francis, formerly Chief Executive of its District Council.

For evidence of Yorkshire reactions to the 1974 changes my debt naturally lies closer to home. It will be clear how very much I owe to the Editors of the Yorkshire Press for permission to consult records and to quote from their columns — more especially those of the *Yorkshire Post*, the *Yorkshire Evening Post (YEP)*, the *Craven Herald*, the *Beverley Guardian*, the *Driffield Times*, the *Whitby Gazette*, and the *Hull Daily Mail*. Cliff Megson allowed the use of a number of his photographs and the Yorkshire Dialect Society allowed a quotation from their "Transactions". More direct impressions of people's responses have come from individuals in various groups and societies, most of whom have supplied documents as well as oral evidence. Among those I should name here are: Ian Alexander (Guisborough), Geoffrey Clarke (Woodlesford), John Fisher (Leeds), Peter Hargadon (Grimsby), Colin Holt (Fenwick), David Isger and Nancy Walsh (Sedbergh), Trevor Pearson (Bridlington), Michael Peck (Beverley), Wynne Smith (Hutton Buscel), Valerie Starsmore (Loftus), Audrey Totty (Hawksworth), and Nigel Wilkin (Yarm). On national matters — especially the status of local government Acts — I have been helped in many ways by Father Francis whose own forthcoming book "The strange case of the Counties that didn't Change" (obtainable from ROOTS (Retention of Our Traditions), 48 Shalmarsh Road, Higher Bebington, Wirral, Cheshire L63 2JZ) sheds important light on the current status of non-administrative counties in England and Wales.

Lastly I record warm thanks to my wife Eveleigh who, though a committed southerner, has devoted much time to reviewing an alien text and helping to make the rough places plain.

Michael Bradford

DISLOCATION

I take a tea bag out of the carton and read what it says on the cover: *Yorkshire Tea blended in Yorkshire, to suit Yorkshire people and Yorkshire water. One bag makes two cups of Yorkshire tea.* In the background are pictures: a shepherd and his sheepdog in front of Whitby Abbey, a batsman, York Minster, the fishing harbour at Staithes, a brass band playing in a limestone dale, and a waterfall.

I don't know whether this is meant to be funny — you can often take Yorkshire chauvinism either way. I can, however, affirm that the bags have often been used with the inferior water of the Thames Valley to produce a drink acceptable to mere southerners.

But that's not the point. What matters is that a place is here being used to exploit people's feelings towards it. The advertisement isn't mainly about the place: it's about the feelings.

And so with this book. It is not yet another volume praising Swaledale and Roseberry Topping, Castle Howard and Bishop Burton. Its starting point is rather that so many other books have done so, that people are fond of familiar places, especially the ones they are brought up in. It is about roots and identity, about the link between people and geography. And if Yorkshire is the chosen example, it is because it is the place I know best, and because it has provided so much evidence of the power of a place and its name over the people who live in it.

It has to be about local government too, but only because the 1972 Local Government Act launched such an assault upon English and Welsh places and names. The critical moment was 1st April 1974 (All Fools Day). *A County vanishes in its sleep* commented the Yorkshire Post. *Thirty thousand people went to bed in the tiny county of Rutland last night and woke up in Leicestershire.* In this dramatic way it described the jolt felt by many up and down the country as the Act was implemented. Huntingdon was lost in Cambridgeshire, Westmorland and Cumberland in 'Cumbria'. Other new counties were invented: 'Avon', embracing parts of Somerset and Gloucestershire, and 'Merseyside' (parts of Lancashire and Cheshire). Whole towns 'moved': Hampshire places like Bournemouth and Christchurch, found themselves in a new 'Dorset'; Wantage and Abingdon left Berkshire for Oxfordshire. In Yorkshire most of the East Riding became part of a new phenomenon, the County of 'Humberside'; part of the North Riding passed to 'Cleveland'; and by smaller peripheral excisions, Sedbergh went to 'Cumbria', Upper Teesdale to County Durham, Bowland and West Craven to Lancashire and Saddleworth to 'Greater Manchester'.

At least for local government they did. And for some that was the end of the matter: those areas were no longer in Yorkshire at all. Others insisted that the changes were only for local government. Yorkshire was a place: Local Government Acts couldn't rename places.

Others, again, didn't care. Not everyone feels a sense of place, and even for those who do a county is not part of it. 'Wake up Warrington' was the challenge of the local paper to the apathy it found in a place destined for a new Cheshire, a town seemingly as 'Lancashire' as Oldham, Wigan and Rochdale whose rugby league teams played its own (and which were also now to 'move').

In Yorkshire, predictably, many did care. *You can call me a Yorkshire nationalist,* said the skipper of the Humber Ferry (born in Hong Kong) as the news about Humberside broke. *The new county plan will leave us stateless. Yorkshiremen will have their nationality violated,* said a councillor when Beverley Town Council debated the matter. Strong stuff — too strong taken literally — but the speakers were not joking.

As we shall see, there were those who acted as well as caring... with petitions, referenda, publicity events and so on. A 'Yorkshire Day' was started. Action groups and societies were formed. Motivation was often not political: it had more to do with identity: *If I can get them to change the name I will die happy,* said a Bridlington councillor.

Many people responded... we are not dealing with just a few cranks. Thousands have demonstrated place-loyalty[1]. It counts towards people's sense of well-being. And we have, in consequence, a problem. Social developments may suggest local government reform every twenty years or so....in the interests of efficiency, an objective all would support. But we do not want the names of familiar places to change. They belong to the land we live on, as we ourselves do.

So with the counties of England. Four hundred years ago, on the first-ever county maps, they had mostly the same names and covered much the same ground as they still did in 1973. And Christopher Saxton was only depicting then what had already existed for hundreds of years before his time. Small wonder that counties were long seen by many as places where people lived, from which they 'came', to which they 'belonged', a focus of regional pride. For centuries they had constituted the very shape of our country, charting our business journeys, our holiday trips, through it as faithfully as the months guide us through the seasons of the year. The 1972 Act, by contrast, was about politics. It answered the question *Into what areas shall England be divided for government – for government by county councils?* But such councils, unlike the counties themselves, had existed for less than a century. Yorkshire as a whole had never had one.

No wonder people were, and are, confused. Did Saxton's Yorkshire — their familiar place — exist any more? Responses differ. Some, Nelson-like, hold the telescope to a blind eye as HMS 'Humberside County' lies anchored in port. Nothing basic, including the East Riding, has changed according to them ......any more than a room's shape really changes if you only move the furniture. Others see it differently, especially if they are politicians...'Goodbye to Yorkshire' is the title of Roy Hattersley's charming eulogy, published in 1976.

We shall note which ways the wind is blowing....increased use of new county names outside local government, instances where Yorkshire overrides them. In a sense the answer to the question is personal. Places persist when people feel them to do. Many would echo Willie Riley, popular novelist of the early 20th Century, self-exiled in Westmorland long before today's dislocations: *Yorkshire has my heart to the end of the way.* For older people that says it all. But the continued survival of a place depends in the end on what society at large does with it, and the future is all unknown.

There is no doubt what most people want, and not just Yorkshire people. They sometimes put it strongly. *The Yorkshire of this book* writes one[2], *is not the mutilated county of the reviled 1974* (sic) *Act but 'Greater Yorkshire' – the Yorkshire of tradition, of county cricket, of centuries of a common heritage and manner of speech that is essentially English but within England unique.* According to this there was indeed change, 'mutilation' even, but the three areas on which Parliament deigned to bestow the name are not the real thing. They are 'the Yorkshires' of politics: 'Greater Yorkshire', on the other hand, is no more, and no less, than Yorkshire as it has always been.

It is, of course, a big place, a 'region' even. *It is now* says Hollingsworth, *like East Anglia, the West Country, the Home Counties, an area that defies strict bureaucratic delineation but is nonetheless unmistakably itself.* There are prouder comparisons abroad — the former French province of Normandy, for instance, which has survived for centuries outside politics. How, indeed, could it fail to do so when the symbol which is its name is sunk so deep in its landscapes and in the hearts of those who love it?

'Love'. This is indeed a book about feeling: the love of places and their names, of the two-dimensional pictures of places we call maps; and in some, no doubt, an associated, mostly harmless, love of self as well. It is not, of course, restricted to Yorkshiremen, though they have been possessed of a remarkably large share of it; nor need it be directed solely to one's own. For many, wherever they come from, it is the old map of England as a whole they treasure, each line and name precious in its familiar place. I count myself among these.

This then is really for anyone who cares, whatever the place, or places, they care about, whether Wantage or Warrington, Oakham or Oldham, Beverley, Bournemouth or Bath.

FOOTNOTES

[1] Like the most recent group, the 'Friends of the County of Middlesex', 22,000 strong in 1987, their first year, claiming support from 24 Middlesex MPs, including the Prime Minister.

[2] Alan Hollingsworth in 'England in Camera colour : Yorkshire' (Ian Allan Ltd) 1979.

CHAPTER I: PLACES AND NAMES

Imagination. I walk down a litter-strewn beach in Limassol, Cyprus, and cup sea-water in my hand; a few dirty drops. Humdrum stuff. And then it strikes me that this is a part, however tiny, of the Mediterranean, and that name, bursting into the contemplation of a drab scene, brings it suddenly to life. For on that featureless grey plain once sailed many who have shaped our civilisation: Phoenicians, Greeks and Romans; Paul, Mark and Barnabas; Turks, Crusaders and Venice, 'holding the gorgeous East in fee'. Here is Homer's 'wine-dark sea', even if it wears a different hue today.

So, through imagination and memory working on a name, can we recreate whole worlds, whole centuries, with a thimbleful of brackish liquid. 'Mediterranean' is that which links this shabby shoreline, and me with it, to our common past.

The feelings places give rise to, through the medium of names, is our subject; more specifically, so to feel a place, its people, its associations, that seeing it, or its name and shape on a map, stirs you, like recognising a person.

You don't even have to have been there to experience it. Listen to a distant worshipper of Yorkshire writing in 1855: *Long before my eyes rested on the mountains of the north of England, the mighty form of Ingleborough was engraved on my imagination by many a vivid description; and when I crossed the old Gothic bridge, and beheld the glorious church, which is the pride and veneration of Yorkshire, it was but the realisation of a long-indulged dream of boyhood*[1].

Belonging. Of course I didn't 'belong' there in Cyprus any more than Phillips belonged in York or the Pennines. The relationship with place was a distant one; hats tipped well back on our heads we gazed in awe across the intervening space. But when people write about their own place there is no gap: they are writing about themselves.

Here is a Yorkshireman[2] describing his Wharfedale home at twilight: *Reek of the hay steals over Threshfield village. The corncrake has gone to bed, but owls are busy with their hunting cry. Quiet and fragrant, urgent with thanksgiving, the White Rose of Yorkshire speeds its message from the garden near at hand.....It is a beguiling homeland to live in, and to know by heart. That is the Rose's call to Evensong.*

Too self-consciously poetic, perhaps, for the late 20th Century, such language, but the feeling of close intimacy and pride is unmistakable. And so is the importance of a name and a symbol as he writes of : *the Yorkshire Rose – the white rose, honey-hearted, that is ours.*

9

"The mighty form of Ingleborough." Photo by courtesy of Cliff Megson.

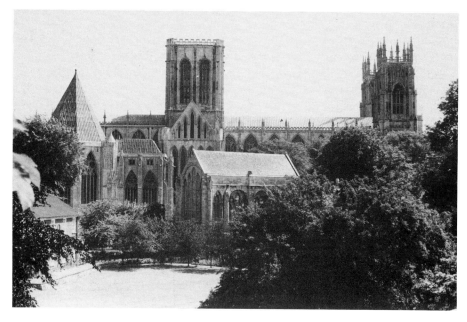

York Minster – "The glorious Church." Photo by courtesy of Cliff Megson.

Then a Yorkshirewoman, intellectual and cosmopolitan, yet acknowledging a primitive rootedness in the old fishing port of Whitby which fixed her being for life: *Of the uncounted places I have lived in, ... only one haunts me. Since I left it for good, I have been adrift and shall drift to my death....* But there is also a link with a past beyond her own, through St. Mary's, brooding protectively over harbour and town. It is a reminder that our precious places, as they outlive us, so they unite us with those who have gone before, and draw a life of their own from those they have sheltered. Note how the body's bones and the building's timber seem almost to fuse in weird communion : *This Church... speaks to my skeleton, which remembers clearly the worn places in stairs, the grain of old wood, the moment – each time as piercing as the first - when a man, crossing the moors above Sleights, sees the sea ... the edge of the cliff, and the church kneeling on it beside the ruined Abbey....how could it forget since those who live in me – and live nowhere else – have stared at it from the moors, from the harbour, from the sea for eight hundred years?*[3]

Motherhood. Belonging, in space and time. Down the long reaches of the centuries place and people are one. The relationship is mutual. Not only is it their place : they belong to it. In the square of Creully, a northern French village, stands the customary memorial to the fallen bearing an inscription as brief and simple as it is moving: *Creully à ses enfants, morts pour la France.* 'Enfants'. Men mature enough to die for their country, are nevertheless children of the village that has given them birth, reared them, mourned them, and is now proud of them. And that village is 'she', not 'it' — ordinary enough, but a living entity, seen as a whole — her sons and daughters, her street, her square, her church, her farms, her hotel, her café. She is much more than what we presently experience: the mere walls and pavings, the people and the cars. She is the thoughts folk have of her, and have had through the years. She is her cemetery, the people buried there and the feelings that gather round them.

But on that memorial two places are spiritualised — one tiny and ordinary, the village herself, the other, one of the grandest 'beings' of all — France, in all the vastness and variety of her landscapes, her culture and her history. France, like Creully, is 'she', which reminds us that the places where we feel rooted can be small, like Threshfield, Whitby, Creully, or large, like France — or Yorkshire. When William Smith, writing a hundred years ago[4] wanted to express what Yorkshire meant to him and his contemporaries and ancestors, there was only one image whereby to express the relationship. She, Yorkshire, was:
   the mother of children who have loved her with a passionate regard.
The fact that we would no longer dream of personifying our places in this way, except, maybe, the country as a whole and only (significantly) in wartime, is a symptom of the problem underlying this book.

Possession. Not that feeling for place has gone altogether — least of all feeling for Yorkshire. The early 1980s saw a group of authors identifying with it so closely as to claim it as their own, and using exactly the same form of title in order to do so: 'Fred Trueman's Yorkshire', with Don Mosey as co-author

(Stanley Paul and Co 1984), Headingley-born traveller-writer 'John Hillaby's Yorkshire' (1986), and in-between, a Cheshire man with a Welsh name, steeped now in the lore and landscape of an adopted home — the 'textile Pennines' — revamping his 'Millstone Grit' in 'Glyn Hughes's Yorkshire' (1985). Three books in three years. Was some sort of competition going on? Not really: the county was big enough for them all; and so, no doubt, is the market.

For the fashion was set by an earlier writer. Paradoxically, if Yorkshire's fame now spreads wider, on both sides of the Atlantic, than ever it did before 1974, it is mainly through the work of a Scot whose country-vet stories breathed such a spirit of wonder at the landscape in which they were set that it was no surprise to find him writing later about that too. The very title 'James Herriot's Yorkshire' (Michael Joseph 1979) suggests closeness, intimacy. He has appropriated the place to himself; and equally he is in bondage to it, the dear environment and the very idea of it. He scatters its name throughout the text as a guarantee of value like the carat-rating of gold. The dark water of the Swale in a gorge, near Gunnerside, is *a real piece of Yorkshire*. West Burton is *a classical Yorkshire village*; even the weather is labelled — *the biting Yorkshire wind* — the people, *those old Yorkshire farmers were a hardier type than city-bred me*, and their food, *Yorkshire fare*. As for the sight of new-born lambs, *it is Yorkshire at its best*.

It is as though the name permeated every living thing and every natural feature, each tree, each stone, each breath of air so that any attempt to prise it away, to change that name, might risk changing the very objects themselves.

Separation. Change. When people and places can be as close as this, as Creully to her children, as Sutcliffe and Herriot to their home ground, no wonder separation causes pain: and so does even the threat of it. It comes in various forms, death, such as befel those French soldiers; occupation by an enemy which they died to prevent; removal to another place; and changes which feel like separation — a new appearance, a new shape, a new map, a new name. As it happens, most of the places Herriot writes about are in an area which the 1972 Act decreed should be called 'North Yorkshire' for local government. It might not have been so. Whitby 'escaped' from an administrative area now called Cleveland only by means of a public outcry based on just those rooted feelings described above. 'My Yorkshire and Cleveland' would have been a less trenchant title for a book. It would also have contained a redundancy, since the real Cleveland is part of Yorkshire. And it would have been confusing because it mixed physical and social geography (Yorkshire) with politics. There are many photographs, in his book, of places Herriot fell in love with — Harrogate and Scarborough, Rievaulx and Byland, Thirsk and Coxwold. County Hall, Northallerton, though a fine building, is not among them.

Nor does it appear in Fred Trueman's book, though this touches every part of the geographical county, with sections on 'Eastern Yorkshire', for instance, and Hull and Middlesbrough cricket grounds. The spectre of separation flits momentarily into its Introduction only to be exorcised with characteristic truculence: *according to the Department of the Environment, no such place as Yorkshire exists. There is – a modern atlas will show – a collection of autonomous*

Wharfedale: "a beguiling homeland". Photo by courtesy of Cliff Megson.

In Coverdale: James Herriot's Yorkshire. Photo by courtesy of Cliff Megson.

local authorities known as North, South, and West Yorks, Cleveland and Humber-side, but there is nowhere that is simply called 'Yorkshire'. Well, that may satisfy the bureaucrats and the cartographers but it cuts no ice whatsoever with around 3½ million men and women who regard themselves as Yorkshiremen and York-shire women and that figure includes the authors (Clearly only adults are meant: the Yorkshire of their book has five million people).

Such feelings having been vented, the place whose existence the DoE and the map-makers had decided to cancel proves here, and elsewhere, to be a living subject just as real as the love which prompts the writing.

'Exile' — the Yorkshire Societies. The day the Times reported Storm Jameson's death it carried an interview with a Doncaster man who had made good in 'Silicon Valley', California, after a stay of many years. Would he become an American citizen? was the question. No, was the answer. He was a Yorkshire-man; why would he want to change? And this to a London paper, not the Yorkshire Post.

When you leave a place altogether, separation is no spectre: it is real. It is also a test of the relationship between you and it. For many Yorkshire people the response is to take what you can with you; and since they cannot take the place, they do the next best things; they take familiar names[5] and, like the Scots and the Welsh, they get together with their kind. On the north wall of the nave of York Minster the observant visitor will read: *This window was replaced in 1948 by past members of The Society of Yorkshiremen in Bombay as a lasting reminder of the good fellowship which prevailed amongst them during their sojourn in India.*

Bombay — New Delhi and Calcutta as well; and Calgary, Vancouver, Queensland, Malaya, Auckland, Uganda, California and so on, all of them societies at one time linked with the one in London.

J. S. Fletcher ('A Book about Yorkshire' 1908) describes the tendency with the swashbuckling complacency of the Edwardians : *The Yorkshireman's first care on settling anywhere is to gather his fellow-Yorkshiremen about him, to make with them a close corporation or society. Other men seeking foreign parts – and it must be remembered that, to the true-bred Yorkshireman, Lincoln and Dublin are just as foreign as Hong Kong or Chicago – are gradually assimilated by their surroundings: the Yorkshireman either converts his new surroundings to his own use and his own likings, or goes elsewhere, undisturbed and unashamed.*

The smugness, perhaps, reads insufferably 80 years on — part of an image to be lived down — but the 'Yorkshire Society' remains a feature of many British towns, even in the television age. I spoke to members of ten — having made contact with twice that number — in places as far apart as Southampton and Stirlingshire, Torquay and Tyneside. I wanted to discover from these 'separated' people how they saw their old place and its name. What did 'Yorkshire' mean to them?

An interest in people and place was implicit in the membership qualification. Birth in the County, descent from a Yorkshire parent, marriage to a native, or a special connection by residence or work were typical criteria. As far as I could see, no language barrier was raised, though the Peterborough Association's motto — *Tak Hod An Sup Lad* — required a measure of reading fluency. I asked them to consider ten possible aspects of Yorkshire and rate their importance. 200 people responded, with the following result:

Aspect of Yorkshire .... Importance rating

People 84%
Countryside, in general 75%
Food 69%
Accents 68%
Particular places 66%
Sport 61%
Rivalry with the South 51%
Rivalry with Lancashire 39%
Music 38%
Local government 19%

(The ratings are a product of the number of people choosing an item and 'mark', on the range 1 — 3, they gave it).

There are few surprises here. The importance of people is confirmed — and of place, with two options scoring well. (Many mentioned the dales and moors). This is in fact the Yorkshire of Herriot and Trueman, with local government nowhere. Very few think of it when they think of Yorkshire. Ironical indeed that it should be an administrative reform which is tending to blur something they value for quite other reasons.

The reality of this creeping confusion came out through another question. The people who responded came from all parts of the geographical county, including the areas administered by Cleveland, Cumbria and Humberside County Councils. Asked whether, for them, Middlesbrough was still in Yorkshire, as many as 25% said 'no'. For Hull only 4% had doubts, and for Bridlington, a mere 1%. But compare Sedbergh (16%) and Saltburn (15%). The opening words of Alfred Brown's famous 'Broad Acres', a description of the landscape in all its magnificent variety, have an ironical ring nowadays: *Where shall I go to find the real Yorkshire?*

Roots The Yorkshire Societies remind us that people will look back to their origins to find their true identity, as Alex Haley did in the novel 'Roots'. The vogue this enjoyed, not least as a television series, was unsurprising in an age of mobility and rapid change. When many societies are subject to the levelling effects of technology and the 'media', the search for individuality is often, of necessity, a quest backwards. It may be pursued energetically, even frantically, by those who have moved, or been moved, away from their place. Those who feel that their place has itself departed or changed may be no less disturbed. And with reason. Distance from what still exists can be overcome: bereavement is another matter.

And it is people with roots who can best understand the pain of losing them.

15

The Times obituary on Storm Jameson (October 7, 1986) noted that it was her origins in the North Riding, and her separation from them, that enabled her to understand and respond to the suffering of uprooted people in Europe after 1933.

In the same paper nine years before, Bernard Levin had pondered the strength of the bond between people and the place they claim as their own, even in unprepossessing spots like the Gorbals of Glasgow and the Falkland Islands. We all had a need, he felt, to be conscious of our own separate existence. We were emotional lightning conductors with mysterious forces flowing through us.....into the earth beneath. Later, the same writer rejoiced at the way ordinary people, both in tyrannies and in democracies, persisted with old and loved names despite all official decrees and regulations to the contrary. His examples were exotic: a New York thoroughfare ('Sixth Avenue') and a Leningrad Opera Company ('The Maryinsky'). By the date of his article, 1987, there were many closer to hand, among the counties of his homeland.

What's in a name? But isn't all this too solemn? What have names to do with roots? The sweet scent of Sutcliffe's roses did not depend on their name. How could Storm Jameson's roots have been affected even if Whitby's own name had changed, let alone the county's? No one really left home that April Fools Day.

But home seemed to leave many of them. It wasn't, of course, just a matter of names, even for those many who cared little about politics — boundary changes seemed to break the ties between people and places. But in any case a name, as we have seen, is not mere scratches on a piece of paper. It is a shape and a sound full of images and the feelings that go with them. Your place is your home, and its name, being part of it, can even become yours: *When I was in the RAF everyone called me Yorkie* said Trevor Pearson from Bridlington, implacable enemy of 'Humberside' — the name, not the local government county.

For Herriot, the word in the title of his book was guarantee of a life extending beyond his own, a way of renewing his own rapturous but finite experience through others: *To my grandchildren, Emma and Nicholas* — ran his Dedication — *in the hope that they will discover Yorkshire for themselves.*

'Yorkshire', in fact, far from being the label on a jar of jam, is the recipe itself.... or at least a shorthand for it.

Images. It is not, of course, just a few hackneyed symbols — a pudding, Ilkley's draughty moor and a song with bumptious tune and gloomy words. Only nine letters on a page, two syllables in the ear, it will evoke a complex vision indeed, and shaken again, kaleidoscope-like, another and more. This one, for instance: an icy breeze on Redcar sands; Pen-y-ghent frowning upon Horton; sadness of lost villages in Holderness; night-long clatter and blaze of wartime lighted mills in dark West Riding valleys; deep splendour of Dentdale, seen from 'the highest station in England'; brass-bands with sound as bright as their names are gloomy — Grimethorpe, Black Dyke; the surprise of Beverley — that other Minster after York (and St Gregory's, Kirkdale, too); Castleford versus Featherstone Rovers; Huddersfield tenors' final F♯ at the end of Sargent's

Messiah; Wombwell slag-heaps; 'Racing at Thirsk'; lushness of the Hodder banks, by Whitewell; Master Cutlers of one great city, and the Town Halls of two others, one a vision of Florence, the other Brodrick's triumphant symbol of local government everywhere; curd tart and parkin; loneliness of Spurn where the Yorkshire naturalists watch; Bainbridge Green; High Force and the Transporter Bridge, symbols of a northern boundary; Kirkbymoorside's market ...and Barnsley's; Holmes and Sutcliffe; the peace of Arncliffe ...of Beck Hole...of Jervaulx; and Kingston (Philip Larkin's 'Here'[6]), proud eastern city of domes and spires (but 'Terry Street'[7] as well), low-built, broad-boulevarded, till now our port through history — but of itself alone, like nowhere else in Britain.

Much is nostalgic (and much is not). Some may even be historical: Fountains and Rievaulx ravaged by agents of the monarch; corpse of Robert Aske hanging on Clifford's Tower, his Pilgrimage of Grace thwarted by the lies of that same Henry — two early instances of Government's dealings with what are sometimes referred to as 'the Provinces'; Guido of York, burned every 5 November...for his foresight? or, more happily, Miles Coverdale, first translator of the whole Bible into English, his place graven in his name (though York also claims him).

The images are personal. How could it be otherwise? *For me, Whitby is Yorkshire*, wrote Miss Jameson. For her friend it was 'glowing gold' of a harvest at Anlaby, and memories of early summer leading her thoughts homewards — *light spray of larches, like green fountains springing among the warm darkness of firs...my heart's in Yorkshire*;[8] and, spite of her own wide and generous convictions, it was the society of her childhood — *granite men and women of the East Riding...clannish to the final degree.*[9] To Herbert Whone, as for many others, the 'Essential West Riding' (Smith Settle 1987) is all millstone grit, chapels and canals, Huddersfield and Haworth (no dales or mountains, no mines or steel).

But it is not just a local matter. Yorkshire's name links you with places and people outside your own neighbourhood. It enlarges your home. It is the Sheffield man's title to 'Brid' and Filey Brigg, for all his delight in the nearby (and Derbyshire) Peak. It is the Humbersider's claim to the North York Moors. It connects us all with everywhere else (and everyone else) insofar as we wish, and are aware; and especially with York, the symbol's ancient origin.

The process of Naming. No wonder there was concern about names in Yorkshire, both before 1974 — among those who were privy to what was going on — and afterwards, among ordinary people. And it was typical of the country as a whole. Names are, of course, as important when you are discarding history as when you wish to retain it. Thus in Africa, colonial 'Southern Rhodesia' becomes independent 'Zimbabwe' — 'Harare' supplants 'Salisbury' as capital. But in England (and Wales) people liked their past, or if they did not, were not going to blame their places for it.

The government had no right to change the names of our native counties, wrote a Cockermouth man, *I was born and bred in Cumberland and I hate the name of Cumbria* (This, nevertheless, being Cumberland's Latin form, used by Saxton on his 16th Century map of the county).

Cumberland's partner, poor Westmorland, sunk without trace from the

Haworth and millstone grit.

map, was restored in 1975 through the renaming of its ancient county town as 'Appleby-in-Westmorland'. *It will show that Westmorland is a place*, said the Mayor. The oddly-named 'Salop' reverted to 'Shropshire' in 1980; and in May, 1984, there was rejoicing in the Hunts Post — *The county paper for Huntingdonshire* — at the local council's decision to restore the old Shire's name, even if it now applied only to a District of Cambridgeshire. In South Wales, sentiment, as well as the needs of tourism, led Preseli District to add the caption: *the Heart of Pembrokeshire* to their franking machine as well as to their brochures. (They had been given 'Dyfed', a word discovered in the cellars of Welsh history. When people do not want change, they may specially dislike the restoration of 'heritage': it adds to the sense of the phoney — see 'Langbaurgh', in 'Cleveland'). As for Rutland, it is a prime illustration of the fact that identity does not depend on politics. Swallowed up in administrative Leicestershire, its citizens, including the District Council, refuse to put that county's name on envelopes and letterheads; and within its 15-by-16 mile area everything possible bears its own name — 'Rutland Knitwear', 'Rutland Launderette', 'Rutland Bookshop', 'Rutland Chinese Takeaway'! and so on. And when authority struck again, flooding no less than a third of the smallest county to form our largest man-made lake, they called it Rutland Water (Officialdom — the Anglian Water Authority — had proposed 'Empingham Reservoir').

If naming was not a purely Yorkshire issue, neither was it confined to the 'provinces' in general or to rural areas where the population is stable and the sense of tradition may be supposed strong. London's own reorganisation had taken place in the sixties, and the same concerns were evident even there. *Countless people bitterly resent the attempts to kill off Middlesex*, wrote a Hounslow woman to the Evening Standard in July 1984, 19 years after the demise of the County Council. *I for one will continue to use the name whenever and wherever possible...We are Middle Saxons, and intend to remain so.* And twenty years before, when the Minister for Local Government had proposed the name 'Kensington' for a new borough which was also to include Chelsea, the latter's Lord Mayor demurred: *This has no chance of willing acceptance in Chelsea* and the press carried pictures of shoppers queueing in the King's Road to sign petitions under the headline: *Chelsea on the March. Don't scrap the name.*[10] In the end the objectors won: 'Royal Borough of Kensington and Chelsea' is the official title.

Double-barrels. Like 'Hammersmith and Fulham', it broke one of the Government's guidelines for names, both then and in 1974, one full of significance for Yorkshire and some of the other counties. *Concocted or double-barrelled names are best avoided*, said the DoE (Circular 58/71). Later on 'Tyne and Wear' broke it too, the new name for the administrative county round Sunderland and Newcastle. 'Tyneside'[11] had been suggested, but Sunderland had pointed out that its own river was not the Tyne. And in the west of England Herefordshire and Worcestershire were united under the label 'Hereford and Worcester', after 'Malvernshire' and a remarkable concoction — 'Wyvern' (Wye + Severn) — had been rejected. (Brilley, a tiny village in the far west of Herefordshire, had actually voted to go into Wales rather than be united with Worcestershire — especially under 'Malvernshire').

There was to come a time when the inhabitants of 'Humberside', remembering these precedents, would propose (unsuccessfully) another name for their own new county: 'East Yorkshire and North Lincolnshire'. For the advantage of such names is obvious. They serve the needs of administration while preserving old identities. That which is one place for politics — 'Kensington and Chelsea' — is clearly two for everything else. Rutland, which had wanted 'Leicestershire and Rutland', noted wryly that, in 1974, the only exception allowed to the double-barrel rule — apart from that watery concoction, 'Tyne and Wear' — occurred in the county of Worcestershire, where the Minister himself, Mr. Walker, was an MP. 'Leicester and Rutland', 'Cumberland and Westmorland', 'Cambridge and Huntingdon' would all have been long names; but scarcely longer than 'Hereford and Worcester',........and no longer than the titles of some pre-1974 counties: 'Cambridgeshire and Isle-of-Ely' and 'Huntingdon and Peterborough'.

Names for Yorks. It is central to this book that Yorkshire is not to be identified with 'the Yorkshires' of local government. It is a mistake to think that Parliament ever considered the ancient county as a whole. Still less did they decide, first to make it smaller and then divide it into 3. They in fact divided it 9 ways (Map 2 Chap. 3). Previously it had had 16 parts (Map 1 Chap. 3). North, South and West Yorkshire came about separately from each other, in area and name. As it happened, all three were eventually given 'Yorkshire' names of the same kind. But there might easily have been only two, or one, or none... in which case the distinction between an underlying place name and political titles would have been clearer.

In the south of the county 'South Yorkshire' was not without a competitor in the quest for a name. 'Hallamshire' had years ago been the designation of an area round Sheffield. Now, in 1971, the Press reported that the name had been suggested, but that the Minister had felt that Yorkshiremen would be up in arms if 'Yorkshire' were to be left out. And so they would, if later experience in the East Riding is any guide — though the proposal had actually come from Yorkshiremen, the Sheffield Chamber of Commerce. Not that this implied a readiness to swap 'Yorkshire' for a new title. More likely it showed that Yorkshire itself was taken for granted — secure enough to need no protection from a mere Act of Parliament.

Further north, the councillors of the North Riding had, not unnaturally, expressed a preference for the ancient term 'Riding' in the name of the new political area. They had to concede, of course, that the original meaning of the term — one of three parts — could not apply to a Yorkshire which was due to be divided into five main parts, as well as bits hived off under 'Cumbria', 'Durham', 'Lancashire' and 'Greater Manchester'. True, 'North Yorkshire' might well be one of only three local government places having 'Yorkshire' in their title; but surely no-one would wish to claim that these places alone made up the real county. (Surely? Too little did we know what was to come). For whatever reason the NRCC's second preference was chosen — North Yorkshire — and the word 'Riding' no longer appears in the official list of the English counties — a fact much lamented by many who see this as its ultimate demise, but not by others who regard it, like Yorkshire itself, as a living term of social and physical geography which no political reform could destroy.

A lesson from Craven. They might well be strengthened in that view by the history of another term now drawn into political service. 'Craven', by which a District was to be known, was already used to denote a socio-geographical area with indistinct boundaries in the west of Yorkshire. Though it had no political significance, its people knew they belonged to it, and their newspaper, the Craven Herald, referred to the various parts of it — such as West Craven and North Craven — in the certainty of being understood. Its capital occasionally wears it for Sunday-best: 'Skipton-in-Craven'.

Those who fear for Yorkshire could take comfort from the survival of non-political Craven up to 1974.

And now it provides an even clearer parallel to the old county's status. For there are two overlapping Cravens, one for politics, with clear boundaries on maps, the other, the old informal one whose western areas are in a District called 'Pendle'. Perhaps, some day, politics will be seen to have supplanted, replaced, destroyed any Craven which is not inside the District. On the other hand the older one may outlive the other. The Herald, meanwhile, still presides over both.

Estuaries. But it is time to turn to the two major Yorkshire estuaries where the largest inroads were made into the political Ridings. The 1972 Act introduced ten new county names to the political map of England, of which half referred to rivers, all but one including the river's name: Tyne and Wear, Cleveland, Humberside, Avon and Merseyside. In each case the two banks of a river were united. There could have been others, but though there was talk of a 'Thames-side' county[12], Essex and Kent, unlike Yorkshire and Lincolnshire, remained, in the end, inviolate. Even the 'Yorkshire' of Scotland, the Kingdom of Fife, came out unscathed a year later, protected, rather than threatened, by its mighty estuaries. And as for the estuary of the Tamar — to the chagrin of Plymouth MP, David Owen, the boundary between Cornwall and Devon remained firm, contrary to all logic, except that of the heart. No such 'sentiment' saved political Yorkshire.

Labels. Consideration of 'Cleveland' and 'Humberside' recalls the world of manufactures, of artefacts, and the closeness of this last word to 'artificial'. The student of local ward boundaries can have no doubt that administrative places are artefacts....convenient sized populations with lines round them. And labels are sought for 'places' just as firms seek a name for the toothpaste or car. But in the latter case nothing fundamental is at stake. Even if a 'brand name' may affect the level of sales, no-one's identity is at risk. And you can even apply 'Cortina' to different shapes and sizes, as one model succeeds another. The fact that it is the name of a real place in northern Italy doesn't matter.

'Cleveland'. In north east Yorkshire such a borrowing happened in 1974: but because the artefact here was a new area, it created difficulties. There was already a Cleveland, an ancient district with ecclesiastical origins, and fine hills — the name's[13] source — on the edge of the North York Moors. Some maps showed it, and they were now going to have to make room for an interloper. There were places in Cleveland — most of the hill country, for instance — which would not be in 'Cleveland'.

Nevertheless the new label solved a problem, partly through what it was, partly through what it was not. What it wasn't was 'Teesside', the name of a county borough, based on Middlesbrough, established as recently as 1968. Throughout the period preceding the 1972 Act people assumed this would be the new county's name. To those, in Yorkshire and Durham, who were threatened with inclusion, the term suggested the flat lands of the Tees estuary, the cranes, the furnaces, the chemicals, the urban sprawl. Many made strong — and successful — representations against such a fate. And there were other conflicting interests at the time, some arguing for a county of different status, others for no county at all.

On to such turbulent waters the new name descended in the Spring of 1972, like the proverbial oil. Vainly did the MP for Hartlepool tell the Commons Standing Committee that 'Cleveland' did not make sense to the Hartlepools, north of the Tees, and would not make much sense to the urbanised area of Teesside north of the Cleveland Hills.[14]

Vainly did Mr. Page, the Minister, seek to champion 'Teesside'. To the MP that was worse still — that was just reverting to the past, if the recent past. He offered, instead, 'Teesport'. Artefact indeed!

The fact is that, with 'Cleveland's' arrival, the new area, its boundaries and its status were soon agreed; and the name evidently helped. It is euphonic, it suggests peace, the countryside, the hills. It has connotations of history and continuity. It is not even without overtones of trade and industry for it was Cleveland's ore that came to the riverbank. Without Cleveland there might have been no Middlesbrough, no Teesside, no County. And maybe it served to reassure, if but slightly, some of those northern Yorkshiremen who were fated to enter the new administrative area. As for those who 'escaped' into 'North Yorkshire' — the folk of Stokesley, the Aytons, the Worsalls — it was from something called 'Teesside' that they thought they had escaped. Did any have second thoughts when they heard that the new name in fact was one which belonged to them? More likely they were outraged.

'Humberside'. Since it is geographically descriptive, 'Humberside' goes back a long way. John Cary's map of the East Riding, 1787, shows, just to the south of Patrington, and on the shore of a river which then flowed round Sunk Island, a tiny village with the name; and a gazetteer of 1808 mentions it. Later it disappeared from maps only to achieve resurrection, and far grander scope, this century. By the 1960s, it was being used — in the phrase 'Yorkshire and Humberside' — as a means of linking the ports and industries of north Lincolnshire with their north bank counterparts for census reports and economic planning.

Unfortunately, it now covers such a large area that it conceals the location of places which it is supposed to label. For as an indicator of place it is precise — so precise that people will often use with it the preposition 'on' — meaning 'by the river' or 'on the riverbank'. Indeed the phrase 'on Humberside' slips out even when they seem to be referring to the whole County. But, again like Cleveland, it has been borrowed for wider use than its strict sense allows; and famous Yorkshire places like Flamborough Head and Bridlington are nowhere near the River Humber. They are thirty miles away. The only 'side' they are on is the seaside.

Joker in the Pack. It was at the end of 1971 that 'Humberside' emerged by stealth, a kind of joker in the pack, an inevitable name for a county which till then had not been expected. People were looking the other way. That for which they were seeking a name was County No.8 in the Government's White Paper, an area north of the river, mainly Hull and the East Riding. And the city councillors of Kingston-upon-Hull were in no doubt what to call it. Having considered 'East Riding', 'East Yorkshire', and 'North Humberside', they unhesitatingly chose 'Hullshire' — the name of a former Wapentake in the area. After all, they argued, the city had always been a county in its own right; and Derbyshire, Leicestershire, Lincolnshire — and even Yorkshire — had been named after the chief city long ago.

Not much Yorkshire patriotism in that choice. Not much sensitivity to the feelings of Yorkshire folk outside Hull either.....though one Councillor was reported as hoping they wouldn't mind. It was a forlorn hope. Beverley Council were unanimous for 'East Yorkshire', its Chairman describing the 'Hullshire' proposal as 'piffle'. Driffield agreed. Had the Hull people their tongue in cheek?, asked one member. *With very great respect...they are not buying a piece of back garden...they are becoming partners in a greater enterprise.*

It was all beside the point. Within weeks the Driffield Times was shrieking 'New county is to be known as Humberside'; and the county to which it referred straddled, contrary to all expectation, the Yorkshire and Lincolnshire shores. Given this, the use of either of these two county names on its own seemed out of the question.

Not to some Yorkshire diehards, though. *Sir....many of us have lived in East Yorkshire all our lives and are very proud to be 'Yorkshire'. There is to be a North, a South and a West Yorkshire. Surely logic must prevail and the proposed Humberside county be called 'East Yorkshire'....* This Driffield Times correspondent, an East Riding County Alderman, proceeded to suggest that his readers simply write to the Minister: 'Please change the proposed name 'Humberside' to 'East Yorkshire'.

The naivety of this was only equalled by its sheer neck. If it was 'logic', it was Yorkshire logic. Perhaps the writer had not noticed that part of Lincolnshire was involved. It may, in fact, be a common assumption among Yorkshiremen that those who do not, as yet, bear their name are only waiting for a chance to do so....To the feelings underlying such a view we now turn.

FOOTNOTES

[1] J Phillips 'Yorkshire' (John Murray 1855).

[2] Halliwell Sutcliffe 'The Striding Dales' (F. Warne 1928).

[3] Storm Jameson 'Journey from the North' (Collins 1969).

[4] W. Smith 'Old Yorkshire' (Longmans 1881).

[5] Within a short space from Toronto Airport you may pass through 'York' to 'Pickering', 'Scarborough' and 'Whitby'.

[6] P. Larkin 'The Whitsun Weddings' (Faber 1964).

[7] Douglas Dunn 'Terry Street' (Faber 1969).

[8] W. Holtby 'Letters to a Friend' (1937).

[9] Vera Brittain 'Testament of Friendship' (Macmillan 1940).

[10] See G. Rhodes 'The Government of London' (Weidenfeld and Nicholson 1970).

[11] Together with 'Bede' and, facetiously (I assume) 'Geordieland'.

[12] In House of Commons Standing Committee B, 18 Jan 1972.

[13] Roughly, it signifies 'cliff-land'.

[14] In Standing Committee D 25 Jan 1972.

CHAPTER 2: PEOPLE AND PRIDE

(i) The 'Difference'

A brief discussion between a Yorkshireman and a Scottishman (sic):

Yorkshireman: I am a true Yorkshireman born and bred, I care not who knowes it. I trust true Yorkshire never denies his county.

Scottishman: I thought you looked like a subtle blade. Date 1650.

God, as they have always suspected in the Ridings, is a Yorkshireman.

Yorkshire is not quite a nation, though we shall find that word being used of it, and not by a Yorkshireman either. But many of its people have certainly regarded themselves as special. The second quotation — a newspaper reporting that a Barnsley man was taking the part of the Almighty in a morality play — makes the point. The first, 335 years older, shows it has been true for a long time.

Outsiders have tended to agree that Yorkshiremen are different. Disagreement has only occurred on whether the difference was in their favour. The Oxford English Dictionary has a 34-line entry about the use of 'Yorkshire' to refer to character. No other county has such an entry. The examples — often referring to cunning and sharp practice — go back to the early 17th Century. They are all unflattering.

A Developing Image. Experience, however, has varied. Two Sixteenth Century quotations could be about today's County Cricket Club. *There be such a company of wilful gentlemen in Yorkshire as there be not in all England beside* wrote the Abbot of York in 1556; and twenty years later, things had not improved, the Archbishop of York observing of 'the Yorkshire race' that *A more stiff-necked, wilful or obstinate people did I never know or hear of.*

Some later visitors, however, had an easier time of it — or were more tolerant. Cobbett, writing in the early 19th Century, was an admirer. He was sure that the hardness and sharpness ascribed to Yorkshiremen arose *from the envy excited by that quickness, that activity, that buoyancy of spirits, which bears them up through adverse circumstances, and their consequent success in all walks of life..*

The Rev. Baring Sabine-Gould, a Cornishman, was evidently forearmed, as the author of the hymn 'Onward Christian Soldiers', against any trouble from his Horbury flock, but spent, in fact, *some of the happiest days of my life* amid *kindness and hospitality.* He found plenty of distinctiveness, of course — indeed he proclaimed every other Yorkshireman to be a character: *No other county produces so much originality,* and eccentricity was the subject of his book, but it was all very affectionate. He offered 'Some Yorkshire Oddities' (pub. Hodges 1874) *as a humble contribution to the annals of the greatest, not perhaps only in extent, of our English counties.*

The experience of another late Victorian cleric was also very different from that of his 16th Century counterparts in the City of York: *I cannot bring to the subject the ardent feelings of a compatriot, but I cannot refrain from loving the county of which my father was a native, and which has given to his son many a kind friend besides.* So spoke James Raine, Canon of York, to the Yorkshire Archaeological Society in 1870; and so kindly-disposed was he to his audience that he ascribed to Yorkshiremen a most unwonted characteristic. When the time came to publish their researches he was sure that *whatever the expense may be...in so free-handed ... a county as Yorkshire the necessary funds will be provided.*

There is admiration here, even affection. In Victorian times the Yorkshire theme was clearly a wholly serious one, and if Yorkshiremen took themselves seriously they were evidently right to do so. A century later the tone has changed. Even among the staunchest 'patriots' a gentle humour laps the rock of their lofty subject. In the Ridings Society's Journal for example: *Yorkshire, the greatest county in the known Universe; the chief merit of the Humber Bridge – to allow less privileged Lincolnshiremen easier access to it –* and *Yorkshire has nothing to do with Camelot. For one thing, no self-respecting Yorkshireman would throw away a perfectly good sword.* (Roy Hattersley on the pragmatism of his compatriots: in 'Goodbye to Yorkshire', Gollancz 1976). Local press reports of the 1971 Local Government White Paper conveyed an even more jokey mood. County pride here reaches the level of farce: Headline — *Hey Up! They want to rive Yorkshire i' bits!...* and then *Dost 'a see what they're doin', lad? Politicians is giving bits o' Yorkshire away, and to them queer folk ower t' other side o' t'Pennines, an' all......what an opportunity for missionary work – for Yorkshiremen to fortify and civilise underdeveloped counties!*

We are a long way here from the respectful tone of Raine and Cobbett. What has happened? First, technology. Since World War II it has created 'the global village'. A hundred years ago the southern Englishman could well have seen far less of Yorkshire and its people than his modern descendant has seen, in the flesh or on the screen, of the United States of America. Now, several times a week we can all sample the processed (and networked) culture of a street in Lancashire, a farm in Yorkshire, a pub in the East End. We can very easily visit the real thing — which may, of course, be different. But the status of regional life declines, along with its mystery, through familiarity real or supposed.

Then there is the history of Yorkshire pride itself. As we shall see, in several individuals it became inflated to the point of self-caricature, a burden which the still proud, but half-apologetic, Yorkshiremen of the late twentieth century find difficult to shed.

The Paragon. In a writer like J. S. Fletcher imagination surely takes over from

25

mere observation in the flush of patriotic feeling:

No Yorkshireman is ever as badly off as any other man – not even a Lancastrian is as resourceful as he.

No Yorkshireman of the true breed ever asks another man to do for him what he can do for himself.

Yorkshiremen as a race hate all oppression and love freedom.[1]

Let us hope that last statement, at least, is true. But note the words 'breed' and 'race'. We shall come to the biological explanations for Yorkshire superiority later on. The 'race', meanwhile, is evidently united to a man in cultural enlightenment: *Every Yorkshireman loves a good picture, good music, a good play.........It is no exaggeration to say of the men of towns like Leeds, Bradford, Sheffield, Halifax and Huddersfield that they are great readers, thinkers, talkers.*

When, regretfully, he identifies a flaw in an otherwise glowing portrait, he cushions the blow in advance with language pitched at the heroic level: *The Yorkshireman is a fine specimen of humanity, and a great Englishman, but he has one sad and terrible weakness – an inordinate love of money.*

At one point Mr. Fletcher's use of the humour of exaggeration suggests that he is, after all, in control of his patriotic urges but then he stumbles over a magnificent lump of unconscious irony. *Having been born with the ineradicable belief that Yorkshire is the finest country* (sic) *in the world and that Yorkshiremen are the most capable examples of the human race yet evolved, he has the habit of conveying to outsiders, not always in the most delicate fashion, a suggestion that they themselves, and their opinions, are only worth consideration when his own have taken first place.*

So far, so good. But then.......*It is not to be gathered from these undoubted peculiarities of the Yorkshireman that he is an arrogant, bumptious fellow who has small consideration for others.* No, indeed.

Yorkshire in the Blood. In Fletcher, the Edwardian West Riding was speaking, in John Fairfax-Blakeborough, the North Riding 20 years later. His enthusiasm for the Yorkshire type led him to seek explanations for it in breeding. He offers help to *those who are not of Yorkshire blood to understand the racial pride of those three Ridings ....* Yorkshiremen are *a clan... a distinct type – little understood, often misunderstood by the casual visitor and even the more careful analyst!*[2] (Note the claim to depth and mystery — the distance between visitor and visited. Who were those 'careful analysts'?) John's father, Richard, warned what might be expected: *Pride ....of being Yorkshire bred and born is so strong within my son and me as to be almost fanatical bias.* 'Almost'? His son can speak of *This racial bluntness of our people.........We have the blood of Vikings in our veins*[3] and so on.

But the most remarkable example of a racial 'explanation' of a people and its alleged qualities comes from the East Riding. A distinguished son of Kingston-upon-Hull had written thus about his compatriots for the members of the Royal Society meeting there in 1922:[4] *The principle of heredity determines the development of nations and communities; birth and training tell in the human, as in the horse race though we carefully select and train in the one case and too often neglect to do so in the other.* Could any Nazi theorist have put that better? But see from

26

what remote causes our heroic attributes spring. *So we Yorkshiremen are a mixed race of some of the most virile ethnological stock such as Vikings and sea-kings, and trained to courage and endurance by the ordeal of battles...and still today Yorkshiremen wear on their county emblem the white rose, but never the white feather...* and so on. The climax is reached in a sentence as tall as the story it tells, of: *our strenuous progressiveness and of the clannishness of our county character, coming to us from the times when our ancestors were compelled to stand shoulder to shoulder in constant combat against the fiercest foes, just as much as our patient persistence and persistent patience may be attributed to the mountainous marches and the weary plodding to and fro over the bridle paths of the Pennine Chain and other ranges, of our nearer forefathers alongside the pack horse, which was the commercial carrier of their day.*

The complacency of a man writing in such terms about the group to which he himself belongs is shocking, or amusing, to readers sixty years later. But Yorkshire supremacy and its racial origins was a theme which even a 'foreigner' could address. The following, written in 1875 by a Bedfordshire man educated at Fulneck, near Pudsey, will be read with relish by northerners of today, when the relative merits of South and North tend to be viewed differently: *this strong infusion of Danish blood...still so favourably distinguishes physically and morally the northern from the southern inhabitants of the island. What a contrast between the muscular frame and indomitable independent spirit of a Yorkshire clothier and the slighter limbs and crouching deportment of our southern peasantry.*[5]

Warts and All. It can hardly be the purpose of a book like this to make fun of 'Yorkshireness', still less to belittle it, but the foregoing shows why others have latterly been inclined to do so. Meanwhile racial speculation seems as dubious as the superiority it purports to explain. Certainly there is no one single type, as even the linguists will confirm: the strongest dialect boundary runs through the county, not round it. But in any case not every 19th Century writer was an admirer. Mrs. Gaskell, though London-born, was well acquainted with northerners, having lived for years in Cheshire and Manchester. Yet her well-known account of the men of the Keighley district conveys a sense of shock. Her subject seems as alien as jungle savages:

Even an inhabitant of the neighbouring county of Lancaster is struck by the peculiar force of character which the Yorkshiremen display....from the general success of his efforts he grows to depend on them and to overesteem his own energy and power.......this wild, rough population....their accost is curt.......enduring grudges, sometimes amounting to hatred.....sleuth-hounds in the pursuit of money...........a powerful race — 'race' again! — both in mind and body, both for good and evil.......a stranger can hardly ask a question without receiving some crusty reply if, indeed, he receive any at all.[6]

No paragon here, certainly, and to show that such traits were not of recent origin, she quotes an Elizabethan writer on the moorland dwellers in the parish of Halifax: *They have no superior to court, no civilities to practise; a sour and sturdy humour is the consequence, so that a stranger is shocked by a tone of defiance.* It reminds us of the quarrelsome individuals mentioned above who tormented the lives of the York clerics in the same era.

North and West. For centuries, then, people have claimed to discern common personality traits in the county's population, however improbable such an idea may be. Even an acute and reflective figure like Storm Jameson writes without hesitation about something she calls the Yorkshire character: *the Yorkshire habit of rudeness .....our Yorkshire distaste for officials.* At one point she even ascribes to their common origin an intuitive understanding of a friend: *We are both from Yorkshire and I understood her form of honesty, her form of timidity (more than half arrogance) her form of insanity..........the Yorkshire character ...under that air of shrewd horse-sense..is complex in the extreme, even neurotic, one edge of its violence turned inward.*[7]

Is there validity in such an analysis? We can only note her assumption that there is something to analyse.

Her reference to 'horse sense' comes from the North Riding and is a link with the characters described by the Fairfax-Blakeboroughs. These differ somewhat from Mrs Gaskell's West Riding men. There is the same laconic directness of tongue — 'plain-spoken even to bluntness' — the same devotion to money, the same cautious, practical bent, the same independence of thought and action, the same love of Yorkshire. But where the West Riding men were noted for stubborn truculence towards strangers, the horse-loving men of the North were famous for their double-dealing and astute bargaining power. The phrase 'Yorkshire Bite' was used to denote this. Like 'Yorkers' — not overscrupulous men to deal with — and 'Yorkshire Tykes' — men to be very carefully watched — it was a means whereby others acknowledged a separate identity and Yorkshire people themselves became conscious of one.

But by sheer weight of population the representative Yorkshiremen of the nineteenth and twentieth centuries were not the horse-dealers of the north, but dwellers in the mushrooming urban centres of the south and west — workers in steel, coal and textiles. And it is Phyllis Bentley, not Blakeborough or the dictionary, who seeks to portray the authentic type — in her novels, but also, most comprehensively, in the 'Shell Guide to Britain' (Ebury Press 1969). Here, 70 British counties are described but in only two is the character of the inhabitants given a mention — Pembrokeshire, because some are Welsh stock and the others English; and the West Riding...... because it is the West Riding: *The West Riding character is robust, shrewd, stubborn, sardonically cheerful though not optimistic, plain-spoken when speaking at all, warm-hearted and extremely independent. Perhaps because of their long history as wage-earners in skilled industries, the West Riding people are accustomed to regard themselves as everybody's equal: indeed they think so well of themselves that a stranger has to prove his worth before he is considered an equal. Once he is admitted to friendship, however, he is a friend for life. Tenacity of feeling is preferred in the West Riding to expressiveness, and any affection of effusiveness or superior manners is despised. A broad humour laconically uttered, a considerable respect for that formidable and competent housewife, the Yorkshirewoman, a slightly excessive interest in 'brass' and again – and again – obstinacy, these complete the portrait.*

The Type at Large. And even in the nineteen eighties such pronouncements continue. So, of Castleford's Henry Moore, the great sculptor, on his death: *He was so utterly Yorkshire – craggy, stolid and stone-like. He did epitomise Yorkshire to me* (a comment reported in the YEP). And then, *He's of good Yorkshire stock....blunt, sincere and not generally prepared to reveal his innermost feelings –* this, of a popular comedienne's boyfriend, in a women's weekly (he is from Hull, incidentally). A 'Guardian' reporter, on the taciturnity of Liverpool Football Club's Scottish manager writes *A quiet Glaswegian is a rarity, like a generous Tyke.* Brian Rix the actor (again from the East Riding) is *a characteristically blunt Yorkshireman.* This last term is, indeed, no mere word: it is an all-sufficient explanation for human conduct. Roy Hattersley MP once flourished a cheque for constituency funds at a local meeting. Was this a token of generosity? No. He was late with his dues, as usual. He was, the local agent explained, a Yorkshireman. The 'Observer' having considered whether a misunderstanding could have occurred between officials of two Government Departments, felt bound to discount the possibility: *Ingham, a plain-speaking and direct Yorkshireman, is not a man who wraps up his words*, was the comment. The Guisborough Cricket Club refused to release their star professional from their own cup-tie to play in a charity match elsewhere. *It is sheer adjectival Yorkshire obstinacy* said the Sport Aid Organiser.

Those, including myself, who might shrink from using the clichés of Yorkshireness cannot deny the existence of public figures who appear to embody them. Whether or not they were born that way, having heard what is required, it seems, they are determined to live up to their calling. In show-jumping Harvey Smith from Bingley won a certain notoriety for a truculent V-sign given to the officials of his genteel sport as millions watched; in football, Brian Clough of Middlesbrough showed a bluntness of speech to match his success; Jake Thackray, the entertainer, purveyed with relish songs of an engaging frankness; and in industry, Arthur Scargill, President of the Miners' Union, forthright and careless of establishment opinion, led workers who themselves, particularly in his own Yorkshire area, displayed an authentic obstinacy and determination throughout the 1984/5 national strike against pit closures....and so on. In the world of cricket, one name, that of Boycott, became proverbial for self-regarding single-mindedness; and it is because the club for which he used to play has never lacked strong characters like him that Don Mosey, weary of its internal strife, felt moved to write (in 'Boycott' (Methuen 1985)) *as a race* (!) *we Yorkshiremen are rude, boorish, stubborn, aggressive, argumentative, disruptive, intolerant and just plain bloody-minded.* Hardly a balanced assessment, nor, understandably, meant to be.

So much for the distinctive Yorkshire character. Whether there is such a thing matters less than the fact that many think there is.

(ii) In the group

Exclusiveness is often felt to be important. We have seen the importance of the birth qualification to the Yorkshire Societies; and the County Cricket Club, despite its lack of success since the 1960s, adhered firmly to it in 1982. *Yorks Still*

Gives Nowt Away shouted the Guardian when the members had reaffirmed the principle by an overwhelming majority. And the Yorkshire Post, under the heading *Yorks Will Not Be Invaded* offered reassurance in case anyone had got the wrong idea: *Yorkshire's xenophobia is not particularly selective. It embraces anyone not actually born in Yorkshire and is not aimed specifically at overseas players.....A spokesman for the Commission for Racial Equality said: Yorkshire as a county are perfectly entitled to make their own rules. Yorkshire is not a nation – even if some people think it is.*

On the other hand, the group is not always beyond enlargement in either of two main ways — the adoption of 'Yorkshireness' by those attracted to it, though not born there; and the unofficial co-option, as it were, by Yorkshire-men of others into the charmed circle, by reason of their 'Yorkshire' qualities or connections. The Observer's Cricket Correspondent must have had this tendency in mind when, in the summer of 1985, a Nottinghamshire batsman completed a magnificent Test century at Leeds. *The Yorkshire crowd,* he wrote, *generously applauded one who had at least lived part of his life in Yorkshire and attended Sheffield University* – the important words here, of course, being 'at least' and especially, 'generously'. The applause, after all, was not merely warm, it was a concession: the man, alas, was not quite one of them.

Volunteers. In the last Century Canon Raine was among those happy to choose membership 'by naturalisation'; and the same attitude was still found 100 years on. *Indian Lawyer Dies a Yorkshireman* ran a headline in the YEP. *Mr. Das was proud of his connections with Yorkshire – he lived in Leeds and Harrogate – and he used to say "I am not an Indian. I am a Yorkshireman".* Not 'an Englishman', we observe: the county idea, as elsewhere, replaces nationality. Prominent among the early members of the Society for Yorkshire was a Dutchman living at Thorner. A Welshman from Ebbw Vale teaching at Whitby recalled the 'escape' of Whitby from Cleveland: *We couldn't have that. We wanted to stay in Yorkshire – and to play for Yorkshire.* Another Welshman — small nations value identity wherever they find it — sought membership of the Yorkshire Ridings Society. He was glad to report that in his area: *as far as adults are concerned, the effect (of local government reforms) has been to intensify the feeling of "Yorkshireness' – much as the partition of Poland intensifies Polish national consciousness.* And he gave his Humberside (literally by the river) address as 'Sunk Island nr Hull, East Yorkshire'. The comparison with Poland, made with complete seriousness, is a measure of the power of 'Yorkshireness'.

The co-opted. Others are promoted to honorary Yorkshire status, whether they want it or not. So, of a successful 19th Century Vicar of Leeds, a Yorkshireman wrote: *Not a Yorkshireman by birth, the energy with which Dr. Hook set to work in doing the hundred-and-one things necessary to be done in his new parish was eminently Yorkshire in its force and persistence* — so it was really Yorkshire that did it — *he beat down, by sheer force of character, and by constant unassuming display of those qualities which Yorkshiremen most love – resolution, plain speech and candour – all the strong and even malign opposition.*

In the Bradford Square which bears his name stands a statue to W. E.

Forster, MP for the city and prompter of the Education Act of 1870. Not born in the county, he was excused this failing by reason of his conduct: *His alien birth was forgotten – all his characteristics, his sympathies, his qualities were eminently Yorkshire in essence and manifestation.*[8]

A botanist, embarrassed by the geographical aggrandisement practised by his colleagues — they were in the habit, he claimed, of including in the Yorkshire catalogue marine specimens trawled near the Dogger Bank, 60 miles off shore — once accused them of acting upon the assumption that the North Sea belonged to the County of York. In much the same spirit writers have reached back in time to discover Yorkshiremen, long before Yorkshire or any other shire existed. Thus the Brigantes and Parisi, Celtic contemporaries of the Romans, are described as 'both, brave Yorkshire peoples'. (And the Romans too, presumably, who settled among them and sought to control them?) Similarly though the Venerable Bede (673 - 735) was born too early to have been a Yorkshireman, his claims — or rather Yorkshire's claims to him — were denied only on grounds of residence. Again, the 7th Century Caedmon of Whitby — *there is reason to believe that Caedmon was not a Yorkshireman, but probably a Welshman,* wrote one author sadly.

For a humorous account — intentionally so, this time — of what might be called 'involuntary naturalisation by merit', the reader might consult 'How I became a Yorkshireman', by Patrick Ryan (Muller 1967).

The Group in Action. By 1678 people called Yorkshiremen had existed for many centuries; and in that year occurred an event which showed that the group was not a merely passive community, content to bask in its identity. We have to go outside Yorkshire, to the Church of St. Mary-le-Bow in London where, on 3rd December, John Tillotson, of Sowerby, later Archbishop of Canterbury, was preaching to 'the first General Meeting of the Gentlemen and others in and near London who were Born within the County of York' — his 'countrymen', in the language of those times. *We are, I think, one of the last counties of England that have entered into this friendly and charitable kind of Society; let us make amends for our late setting out by quickening our pace, that so we may overtake and outstrip those who are gone before us: let not our charity partake of the coldness of our Climate, but let us endeavour that it may be equal to the extent of our Country; and as we are incomparably the greatest county of England, let it appear that we are so, by the largeness and extent of our Charity.* The purpose of such anniversary meetings he described as *The maintaining of Friendship and the promoting of Charity.....two of the best and noblest ends that be.*[9]

Charity. As the Epistle Dedicatory makes clear, the occasion included a banquet — the 'York-shire Feast' — the means of 'maintaining friendship', and by 1690 the event had developed to the point where 'a very splendid entertainment of all sorts of vocal and instrumental music' was provided, including — at a cost of £100 — the newly-composed 'Yorkshire Feast Song', words celebrating the 1688 Revolution set to music by Henry Purcell himself. The records do not say how charity was promoted, nor is anything known of the progress of the event in the 18th Century. But by 1812, the Yorkshire Society's School had been founded, implying the prior existence of a Society of some kind at that stage. This school, funded by donations and the annual subscriptions of members, was 'for girls and boys of Yorkshire parentage'. By the 1930s, with increased provision by the state, the School itself had disappeared, but boys with needy parents were still being assisted at Yorkshire boarding schools.

Of most interest here is the link drawn between charity — helping the School — and 'patriotism': *By supporting the charity and interesting themselves in its work they will find a not unworthy opportunity of evidencing that predominant characteristic of a Yorkshireman's heart – love for his native county.* Thus reads an 1891 report which was realistic enough to touch also on an equally characteristic concern: *the economical way in which the school is conducted, by the strict supervision of a practical committee, who maintain the credit of Yorkshiremen for shrewdness and thrift.*

Friendship. Though 'charity' persisted, in the form of the school, throughout the 19th century, the tradition of annual social events had evidently lapsed many years before the founding, in 1899, of the Society of Yorkshiremen in London, a body which was to demonstrate for the next eighty years the prestige and high morale of the County and its representatives in the capital. Confidence, indeed, had prevailed at a banquet which, though it took place 8 years earlier, marked in effect the Society's beginning and the revival of those 'York-shire Feasts' held 200 years before.

Some two hundred gentlemen in evening dress toasted 'Yorkshire our County', 'Yorkshire Members of Parliament', and 'Yorkshiremen in London', (ie themselves and, in those days, an estimated 12000 others); and to make doubly sure of their own prosperity, a member quoted the Cleveland toast — though in a shortened version.[10]

> *Here's tiv us, all on us;*
> *May we niver want nowt,*
> *Noan on us!*

Great enthusiasm obtained the whole evening, ran the report *and the excellent feast of good things on the table, and the choice musical entertainment – thoroughly Yorkshire in its character and performers – were as eminently supplemented by the speeches delivered.*[11]

By the mid nineteen-twenties, and on into the thirties, the Society flourished under the motto 'Tria Iuncta in Uno', with upwards of 800 members. There were the Annual Banquets, 'Bohemian Concerts', cricket matches (in 1923 they lost to the Association of Lancastrians in London by 154 to 102), debates on such themes as 'the natural beauties of the West Riding are superior to those of the other Ridings', lectures ('The Bronte Country', 'The Yorkshire Dialect and its Humour' and so on) and the Benevolent Fund Ball. A typical annual subscription to this Fund from the usually well-off Yorkshiremen who could afford to be in London was 10s 6d. The list of grants from it also reflect another era:

To a Yorkshireman to obtain a pedlar's licence.
To a Yorkshirewoman of good family, a cripple aged 74.
To a Yorkshireman to procure clothes out of pawn and a ticket to Sheffield to
enable him to take up work there.
To a Yorkshire family where the father is in a sanatorium...and so on.[12]

The list of members of the Society is a roll-call of 'the great and the good'. In 1923 the 260 Vice-Presidents included the Speaker of the House of Commons, a Duchess, 3 Marquesses, 5 Earls, 3 Viscounts, 11 Lords — with names like Fairfax, Halifax and Savile — 43 Knights and countless JPs and Lieutenant Colonels. The two Patrons, then and 10 years on, were the King himself, George V, and the future King, the Duke of York (to whom, on the occasion of his marriage with the Lady Elizabeth Bowes-Lyon, the Society presented a Chippendale Grandfather clock and two 'renown' travelling cases — total cost £123-10s). The President was the Archbishop of York. Scanning the membership the eye lights on names like Asquith (the former Prime Minister); Ferens, Wilberforce (Herbert), Rank and Reckitt from Hull; Rowntree and Terry (York); Philip Snowden, Rupert Beckett, Dorothy Una Radcliffe, Halliwell Sutcliffe...each listed with his Yorkshire home town or Riding — (so many from the East Riding).

What would the reactions of such an Establishment group have been to 1974 and its aftermath? A pointless question. The Society of the 1970s, like others in the television age, was a shadow of itself, and by the 80s had foundered altogether.

(iii) The Springs of Pride

One man, from whom we have already heard, would certainly have had something to say, that fanatical patriot, Sir Alfred K. Rollit, LL D., MP. No reform, nor any interpretation of one, which implied that his beloved Hull was no longer in Yorkshire would have been tolerated. As it happened, it fell to him to address his corpulent 'countrymen' with their waxed moustaches at that banquet in 1891; and in doing so he explored the origins of the pride that had brought them there. The year should be noted. Many people 80 years later took too shallow a view of Yorkshire patriotism by ascribing it to success in county cricket. If that had been true, Sir Albert would have had nothing much to say since the first of the Yorkshire Club's thirty championships in sixty-six years — a record unrivalled by any other county — did not take place till 1893, two years after his speech was delivered.

The English Rome. If we are considering feelings that go back centuries we cannot ignore — though Sir Albert did in his speech — the prestige of the place which gave the county its name. Yorkshire, after all, is 'the County of York'. Nowadays Leeds, Sheffield, Bradford and Hull surpass York in importance and have done so for a long time. But we need longer perspectives. Far down the centuries York city rivals London in age and significance. A letter written by Pope Gregory in 601 gave its Bishop equal seniority with the Bishop of London

*Title-page of Tillotson's published
sermon.*

*Chairman's badge of office, the
Society of Yorkshiremen in
London.*

HULL, JULY 1787.

HULL AND YORK
ROYAL MAIL-COACH,
WITH A GUARD,
WELL ARMED.

SETS out every Day about *Half-paft Three* in the Afternoon, from
Mr. *BAKER's*, the *Crofs-Keys*, in the *Market-Place, HULL,* and
arrives at Mr. *PULLEINE's*, the Tavern in *YORK*, in SIX HOURS;
returns from thence about *Half-paft Twelve* at Night, or immediately
after the Receipt of the LONDON MAIL, and arrives at *HULL* early
in the Morning.
No more than *Four Infide* and *Two Outfide* Paffengers will be taken.
    Fare, 10 s. 6d. INSIDE; OUTSIDE 5 s. 3 d.
    Short Paffengers Threepence-halfpenny *per* Mile.
Parcels from 3 d. to 6 d. if above a Stone Weight One Half-
penny *per* Pound.
    For Places or Entry of Parcels, apply to *Henry Cawood*, at the Poft-
Office, *Hull*: Mr. *Pulleine, York*; Mr. *Bland, Beverley*, and to Mr. *Gill*,
King's Arms, *Market-Weighton*, from thofe Towns refpectfully for
Hull, York, London, or *Edinburgh*.
    Conveyance may be fecured for Paffengers and Parcels from *Hull* to
London (Fare 3 l. 13 s. 6 d.) by the MAIL COACH, the whole Way, ex-
cept the Places be previoufly difpofed of at *York*, in which Cafe Mr.
Pulleine engages to fend the Paffengers forward in a Poft-Chaife at the
fame Expence and accompanying the MAIL COACH; the fame from
Hull to *Edinburgh,* 3 l. 13 s. 6 d. or any intermediate Places at Fares in
the Proportion of Diftance.
    * The Proprietors give Notice, that they will not be accountable for any Parcel exceeding
the Value of Five Pounds.

Q

Revelry at Holborn, 1891.

Eighteenth century travel.

(Canterbury's predecessor as Primate).[13] Earlier still, as we shall see, it had been the seat of the Roman Emperor himself. As a symbol of power, spiritual and temporal, it is in the international league with Rome and Constantinople. In mediaeval times men could not have been unaware that here was the heart of one of the two Provinces of the Established Church, here where our largest Gothic building (after old St. Paul's) rode high over rooftops and blocked the view down the twisting 'gates'. In the Ages of Faith they could not have been unimpressed by that fact.

It was the centre, too, of a land rich in the things that counted. In this city, the County's magnificent array[14] of abbeys, churches and castles — Bolton and Byland, Patrington and Pontefract, Selby and Conisbrough, and all the rest — seem epitomised in a great religious and military display.

Broad Acres. Sir Albert, however, ventured to think it was because of its size that Yorkshiremen were proud of their county. It felt larger in his day — before the motor car — than in ours, and larger still in earlier centuries, before railways. You could spend hazardous days crossing it.

We found the way very deep, and in some places so dangerous for a coach that we walked on foot, but the Lord preserved us from all evil accident......blessed be God. So wrote Ralph Thoresby in 1708.... of a journey from Leeds to York!

No doubt England seemed bigger everywhere then, but men had no need to travel to sense the incomparable size of Yorkshire. You could 'see' it, in a new kind of way. For Christopher Saxton's maps — the first county maps of England — appeared in the late 1570s and, as a recent writer[15] put it, he *provided an image of England, composed of separate counties, that helped to shape and reinforce that sense of regional identity and independence for which historians have found so much evidence in their recent research on early modern England.*[16] The title page of Saxton's Yorkshire sheet (1577) reads in Latin *The County of York (whose inhabitants were once called Brigantes), in length, breadth and population more distinguished than the rest.* Note the inflated grandeur of the language; Yorkshire isn't just larger and more populous — this last assertion, incidentally, being open to doubt, — it is 'illustrior'. It reflects the cartographer's justifiable pride in a pioneering enterprise; and it suggests something else. He was himself born near Morley and is basking in reflected glory from his own place.

John Speed, Saxton's great successor, was able to be even more extravagant in his language. For his map of 1627 was accompanied by an extended description of Yorkshire, one of the first that Yorkshiremen would ever have to read — and which many of the well-to-do would certainly have come to know. Yorkshire, for him, is 'this great Province', 'so worthy a country', 'this Nation', 'this great Region': *Yorkeshire, farre greater and more numerous in the Circuit of her miles, than any Shire of England.*

Speed's account also confirms the importance of York to the general image: *Yorke, the second Citie of England...is a singular ornament and safeguard to all the North-parts.* He notes that Constantine was proclaimed Emperor there.... *from whence it may be gathered of what great estimation Yorke was in those dayes, when the Romane Emperour's Court was held in it.* Its religious status is lofty...*For the greater dignitie thereof it was made an Episcopall See by Constantius and a Metropolitane Citie by a Pall sent unto it by Honorius.*

No mean city; and one with which all Yorkshiremen are associated through their name, ever since the first creation and naming of the Shire.

"The first Province of these Kingdoms"[17]. Already, in the late 17th Century, men were glorying in the variety of the County's natural resources and the exploits of its people. George Hickes, the Yorkshireman Dean of Worcester, had drawn attention to both in his sermon at the third York-shire Feast, in 1682: *Our County...is the epitome of England; whatsoever is excellent in the whole land being found in proportion thereto....Besides, God hath been pleased to make it the birthplace and nursery of many great men.*

200 years later Sir Albert Rollit asserted that Yorkshiremen were proud of their mills — *scenes of toil by day or ablaze by night* – and what they produced; of Oastler and Fielden whose statutes had protected those who worked in them, of Captain Cook, of Wycliffe, of Marvell and Wilberforce, of Congreve, and of Priestley and Faraday[18] among scientists. He had even traced the *greatest thinker of this age, Darwin, to descend from a Mayor of Hull! They might well be proud* runs the account of his speech *of the architect of the great Forth Bridge, Sir John Fowler. It was men like those who had made Middlesbrough rise from a village. A great authority* (!) *told him the other day that the three great forces in the world now were Yorkshiremen, Scotchmen and Chinamen – for wherever one went there these three races were – pushing the interests of their country, and displaying the greatest force of character in the pursuit of their ends....* As elsewhere, Sir Albert's feet may seem to have left the ground at this point, but his commitment to the progress of the whole county — a Hull man pointing to the growth of Middlesbrough — contrasts with the mutual indifference (at best) of our cities later on.

Speed had echoed Hickes's other theme: *She* (Yorkshire) *is much bound to the singular love and motherly care of Nature, in placing her under so temperate a clime, that in every measure she is indifferently* ie 'equally' *fruitfull....if one part of her be.... a sandy barren ground, another is fertile and richly adorned with corne-fields...If one place be Moorish, Mirie and unpleasant, another makes a free tender of delight, and presents itself to the eye, full of beautie and contentive varietie. To Yorkshire folk* wrote Harry Scott many years later, *this is a broad land of broad acres, intended by nature to be more than a county, rather a world in itself with a broad diversity which becomes almost self-sufficiency in the essentials of a good life not shared by less-favoured counties.*[19]

Let us leave the theme of Yorkshire pride — insofar as this book ever can — with a hymn of adulation from a time when such feelings were approaching their zenith: *In size larger than many a continental principality; in fertility and wealth of scenery as rich as it is large; the home of empire for many a long century under Briton and Roman and Angle; and then, when at length discrowned, the arbiter and spring of the political power of the country; the mother of children who have loved her with a passionate regard; and who remembered her most when they were greatest themselves – these are things of which any county can be proud.*[20]

FOOTNOTES

[1] 'The Making of Modern Yorkshire 1750-1914'. J. S. Fletcher (G. Allen & Unwin 1918).

[2] 'Yorkshire Days and Yorkshire Ways'. J. Fairfax-Blakeborough (Heath Cranston 1935).

[3] 'The Spirit of Yorkshire' J. & R. Fairfax-Blakeborough (Batsford 1954).

[4] Quoted in 'Hull and the East Riding of Yorkshire'. Ed. T. Sheppard (Brown 1922).

[5] 'Pamphlet on Yorkshire Place-names and Surnames'. J. Shannon, 1875 (quoted in Yorkshire County Magazine Vol 2, ed. J. Horsfall Turner 1892).

[6] 'The Life of Charlotte Brontë'. E.C. Gaskell (Routledge 1905).

[7] Storm Jameson. Op.Cit.

[8] J. S. Fletcher. Op. Cit.

[9] Quoted in Yorkshire County Magazine, Vol.i, ed. J. Horsfall Turner 1891.

[10] A longer one reads: *Here's to me and here's to thee and here's to all on us. May we niver want nowt, noan on us, nor me noather.* Response: *Fond love, owd son.*

[11] Yorkshire County Magazine, Vol.i, 1891.

[12] Annual Report of the Society of Yorkshiremen in London, 1923.

[13] Bede 'A History of the English Church and People' (Penguin Classics p.85).

[14] Wm Smith 'Old Yorkshire' (Longmans 1881) lists 17 Abbeys, 33 Castles.

[15] V. Morgan in "The Geographical Magazine" (March 1980 issue).

[16] The process was assisted by a set of playing cards based on Saxton and published in 1590, each showing the shape, and describing very briefly the general character, of a county — there happened to be 52 counties in England and Wales. It was like a family group, and of course, if one was missing — Yorkshire, say, or Rutland — the pack was useless.

[17] Wm Marshall (1788) on the variety of farming in Yorks.

[18] It was, of course, too early for names like Cockcroft, Appleton and Hoyle to appear in the list.

[19] Harry J. Scott, "Yorkshire Heritage" (Hale 1970).

[20] William Smith. Op.Cit.

CHAPTER 3: GEOGRAPHY AND POLITICS

Since 1974, Albert Rollit's Hull, and the Middlesbrough whose growth pleased him, have been in administrative counties which do not have a Yorkshire name. A list of places to which the same thing happened is shown below. It would have been considerably longer had pride not spurred many to protest about the changes proposed in the 1971 White Paper. Their story is told in Chapter 4.

But strangely enough, pride, or something akin to it, was equally a reason why protest was not stronger. It led many to see Yorkshire as too fundamental to be at risk from an Act of Parliament that was only about local government. They shared the complacency, if not the theology, of Robert Carne, hero of Winifred Holtby's 'South Riding' (Collins 1936): *He worshipped the creator of earth and heaven, the Lord of Harvest, who had in his beneficent providence ordained that Yorkshire should be the greatest county in England, which was the greatest country in the world...* Their place was taken for granted like the air they breathed.

Administration, on the other hand, was a remote subject. We have seen the apathy of the Yorkshire Societies towards it. Researchers reported to the Maud Commission in the late 'sixties that this was typical of the nation:[1] *six per cent of the sample may be defined as interested in elective participation in local government.....There is little conclusive evidence from the results of these questions to suggest that electors care whether public services should be the responsibility of local authorities or of other central bodies.* And the Yorkshire Post, on 19th May 1969, asserted that...*of local government electors who possessed strong opinions, nearly two-thirds desired no change.* So among the few who cared, most were happy with things as they were. Equally, if the changes could have taken place without affecting anything else, they would no doubt have been accepted without fuss.

It was not to be. Geographia Ltd, to quote one example, having previously produced a travel guide called, simply, 'Yorkshire', now brought one out with the strange title 'The Yorkshires and Humberside'.[2] What were people to make of this? Was local government after all so central and powerful as to be able to destroy, or at least to modify, Yorkshire itself? 'The Yorkshires' indeed! According to this a place used to being divided, like Caesar's Gaul, into three parts[3] without losing its integrity, was evidently not to be thought of in that way any more. It was now not one thing, but three; and places which had their services provided by a county council without 'Yorkshire' in its name — like Humberside — were no longer Yorkshire places at all.

Geographical and Administrative Counties. Many disagreed. On 12 August 1979

The Spectator published the following from a Leeds man: *Sir......If the faceless underlings of Heath and Walker thought that by quietly putting a blue pencil through the 1100-year old Ridings it would be the end of the matter they have been sadly mistaken...Geographically the county of Yorkshire still exists in spite of the machinations of Heath, Walker and Co., and by God's grace and the determination of all true Yorkshiremen will continue to do so.*

'Geographically'. The distinction implied by the word used to be well understood. In 1888 the President of the Local Government Board, when steering through the Commons the Bill which first created county councils, was asked why the term 'administrative county' was used. It was to make clear, was the reply, that when speaking of a county they were speaking of an administrative county as distinct from a geographical county — the latter, presumably, being the area which, with relatively minor amendments, had remained the same for centuries, and whose existence, whose 'reality', rested on that. Sixty years on, the Boundary Commission, in its annual report, confirmed the point. 'None at all' would be the effect of their decisions on geographical counties. They were concerned with local government ones. *In Yorkshire,* they wrote, *it has been found proper for centuries to have more than one such area for local administration, but for matters outside local government, and to the world at large all its inhabitants are Yorkshiremen.*[4] As late as 1984, a TV rugby commentator had no doubt about geographical counties. It was the other kind that mystified him. *This match is coming to you from Bath, which is in Avon, whatever that is. The match is between two real counties, Somerset and Yorkshire.*

Yorkshire itself was not needed, before 1974, to illustrate the difference. The Ridings themselves did that. The geographical East Riding was larger than the local government one for it included Hull which governed itself — and was therefore a 'County Borough' (Map 1)[5]. In the West Riding many large towns were similarly independent. If being a West Riding man had meant paying rates to the County Council Bradfordians would not have qualified. But everyone knew that they did. No-one, in those days, confused geography with politics. The notion of a non-political county was not invented by traditionalists after 1974 in order to preserve Yorkshire — it was already familiar.

Yorkshire in fact was a county to which no-one paid rates and no-one ever had. There seemed to be only one kind of Yorkshire, the geographical one. True, at the very start the area must first have been demarcated for the purpose of running it, or at least owning and guarding it; in former centuries it had been the field of operation of a Lord Lieutenant, a representative of the Monarch charged with sustaining military readiness; it had once sent representatives to Parliament elected on a county-wide basis;[6] there had been important county assizes at York. But nothing remotely like the role of present-day county councils had ever been discharged under Yorkshire's banner. Such services as had existed had been performed by JPs organised within Ridings.[7] For a long time before 1974 the one slender claim to administrative status of Yorkshire viewed as a whole rested in the office of a High Sheriff.

The county as a place, meanwhile, seemed guaranteed by natural features: sea, Pennines, Tees and Humber, even if the Tees was not the obstacle it once was and undrained marshlands no longer extended the Humber barrier south-

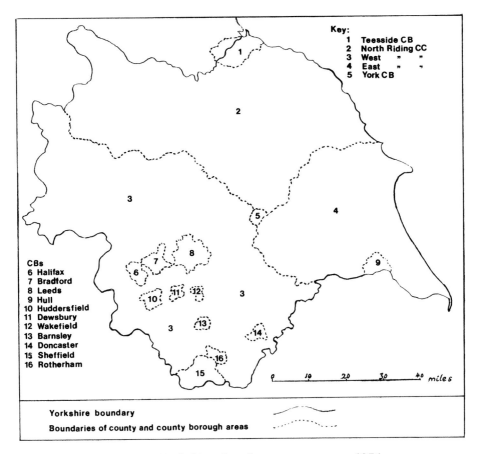

Key:
1 Teesside C B
2 North Riding CC
3 West " "
4 East " "
5 York C B

CBs
6 Halifax
7 Bradford
8 Leeds
9 Hull
10 Huddersfield
11 Dewsbury
12 Wakefield
13 Barnsley
14 Doncaster
15 Sheffield
16 Rotherham

Yorkshire boundary

Boundaries of county and county borough areas

Map 1. Yorkshire: Local government, pre 1974.

westwards towards the Pennine foothills. Most Yorkshire literature, moreover, dealt with scenery and other leisure attractions; even the published histories of the county, unlike those of England, seldom dealt with the topic of its government.

Yorkshire Places administered in Counties without a Yorkshire name:

North Riding	Admin. area
Bowes	Durham County
Brotton	Cleveland County
Guisborough	Cleveland County
Loftus	Cleveland County
Marske-by-the-Sea	Cleveland County
Mickleton	Durham County
Middlesbrough	Cleveland County

40

Redcar	Cleveland County
Saltburn-by-the-Sea	Cleveland County
Skelton	Cleveland County
Thornaby-on-Tees	Cleveland County
Yarm	Cleveland County

West Riding

Barnoldswick	Lancashire County
Bolton-by-Bowland	Lancashire County
Dent	Cumbria County
Earby	Lancashire County
Garsdale	Cumbria County
Gisburn	Lancashire County
Goole	Humberside County
Great Mitton	Lancashire County
Saddleworth	Greater Manchester County
Sedbergh	Cumbria County
Slaidburn	Lancashire County
Whitewell	Lancashire County

East Riding

Beverley	Humberside	County
Bridlington	"	"
Driffield	"	"
Flamborough	"	"
Hedon	"	"
Hornsea	"	"
Howden	"	"
Kingston-upon-Hull	"	"
Market Weighton	"	"
Patrington	"	"
Pocklington	"	"
Rudston	"	"
Sledmere	"	"
Withernsea	"	"

Among natural landmarks, Flamborough Head and Spurn Head (Humberside County), the Trough of Bowland (Lancashire County), Mickle Fell, at 2591ft, Yorkshire's highest mountain, and High Force (Durham County) should be mentioned.

The distinction — the experts' view. No wonder so many were relaxed at the prospect of local government change. It simply wasn't Yorkshire's scene. Those who took the trouble to seek assurances about the county's future were apt to have their slightest worries dispelled. *The broad acres known as Yorkshire will remain unaltered despite the different names adopted by the new* *administrative counties* said a DoE spokesman, quoted in the Times. 'White Rose Ties Hold Firm Despite Amputations' ran the headline.

To a question about "our pride in our county" J. R. James, Professor of Town and Regional Planning at Sheffield University, had replied: *A Yorkshireman will always be a Yorkshireman quite regardless of the administrative map. I am quite sure that the loyalties we have to the geographical county and to the area will not in any way be affected by administrative reorganisation.* (Reassuring indeed, but note the phrase 'the administrative map'. Did he know then that this was to be the only kind of map and that consequently Yorkshire would not appear on any?) *The geographical area* – he went on – *had survived the fact that there had never been a Yorkshire administratively. There was a danger that people would resist change by playing on the fact that they would lose their identity with place. People had never lost their identity with place and never would.*[8]

That was plain enough, and from an expert. Yorkshire was a place, not a political unit, and that was how people would go on regarding it. Derek Senior, a member of the Maud Committee itself, made much the same point in a memorandum which expressed his dissent from his colleagues' main recommendations, and his reason for making it was similar to James's — a desire that changes should be more radical than the Committee had felt able to propose because of its fears about identity. There were two kinds of county, and the one to which people felt loyalty was not the one to which they paid rates. He wrote of *..the fallacy that traditional county loyalties attach to the administrative county. They do not; they attach to the geographical county. The counties of England had commanded the allegiance of their inhabitants for a thousand years before they became service-running agencies, and will continue to do so for a thousand years after they cease to be such.*[9]

And then a statement which was not an attack on local government but only an attempt to put it into proper perspective: *It is only to the members and senior officers of a county council that 'the County' means the area whose services they run.*

Mr. Senior could quote several telling illustrations of the main point: *Three out of every five Lancastrians live in towns excluded from the administrative county of Lancashire, but their county loyalty is not one whit less strong than that of the remaining two. And no county symbol can claim doughtier champions than the red rose – unless it be the white, whose shire has never been an administrative county. Middlesex is just as self-consciously Middlesex as it was a few years ago, when its major services were run from its own Guildhall, and Bromley men remain as obstinately Kentish as they ever were.* (Bromley having achieved London Borough status separate from political Kent). *It is only by a sort of confidence trick that a county council can persuade its electors that their 'county' is threatened with extinction when nothing but its own corporate existence is at stake.*

As we shall see, it was not so much the electors as the Minister himself who was persuaded by such arguments, to the extent that not only did he retain 'counties' in local government but his reforms served to obscure the distinction between that kind of county and any other. They certainly encouraged views widely different from those of James and Senior. When 1974 came along the new County of Cleveland had Yorkshiremen to look after, in the area of the

North Riding, but on the day of its birth its Chief Executive observed: *The difference between the historic and geographic county and the local government one is interesting because parliamentary spokesmen have suggested that present changes are relevant to local government only and that the ancient counties will still remain for such purposes as Wars of the Roses and county cricket. But Cleveland County Council already has its Lord Lieutenant and other features of the historic county will soon emerge. I suspect that after a few generations we shall be Clevelanders all. And why not?*[10]

No doubt there were readers in places like Middlesbrough and Redcar who reacted with indignation to Mr. Woodham's rhetorical flourish at the time but many of the portents were on his side.

The distinction — the official view. First, what were the Government's intentions? Did it have a view on the retention of non-political counties — Westmorland and Yorkshire, for instance — covering the same areas as before, whatever the name of the councils which administered them? The 1972 Act itself stressed that the reforms were for local government. But nowhere did the Act, any more than the preceding Maud Report or the White Papers, deal with geographical counties or the distinction between two kinds. Why should they? Their subject was local government.

But it is not difficult to uncover the unspoken assumptions of Ministers. One clue is indeed something that was not said — unspoken — about the use of new county names by contrast with those of the new districts (the new system was based on districts within counties). For the districts, the Government was careful to distinguish new names from existing ones; and it explicitly stated that the former were not meant to be used outside local government: *while the names in the order apply to the districts defined for local government purposes, they do not supersede existing place names; nor do they affect postal addresses or local usage for purposes other than local government* (DoE Circular 39/73).

This applied to 'Kirklees' and Langbaurgh', 'Richmondshire' and 'North Wolds' and the like. They were not intended to replace names like Huddersfield and Redcar, Catterick and Bridlington. Traditionalists took heart from these restrictions and assumed that they covered the counties as well. They were wrong. No government document attempted to distinguish 'place' from 'local government unit' in respect of 'Avon', 'Cleveland', 'Humberside' and so on. To quote a Department of the Environment reply to my letter on this subject: *the Act was silent on the use of the names* (of the counties) *for the purposes outside the field of local government.*

In the same reply the restriction placed on district names was explained as follows: *since the power to name the districts was derived from legislation primarily concerned with local government, it would not have been appropriate for the Department... to seek to impose the use of the names for other purposes.* This misses the point. The Circular did not merely shrink from imposing the new names; it boldly asserted the limits of their use within the purposes of the Act. But since the power to name the counties also derived from the same legislation, why were no restrictions placed on their names?

The answer lies in the conservative nature of the reforms at county level. 45

county authorities remained, the same number as before (below them, 1158 districts shrank to 332). The threat to Yorkshire arose, paradoxically, from the fact that there was so little danger to most of the other historic counties. In general the old names were retained. Of the 45 only twelve had new ones, including all five which between them were to look after most of Yorkshire; but of these five only two really seemed new: 'Cleveland' and 'Humberside' (Map 2). These, with 'Avon', 'Cumbria', 'Tyne and Wear', 'Merseyside', and one or two others, simply took their place alongside almost all the old ones.[11] And since there was no doubt that the latter — Cornwall, Dorset, Warwickshire, Norfolk and the rest — would continue in use outside local government there seemed little chance of restricting the use of the former. In any case it was not in the Government's interest to try. For whether or not it was the administrative Hampshire or the geographical one which had hitherto focused people's loyalty, the aim of the new arrangements was to harness such feelings to the cause of local government. This was encouraged by the fact that in many cases, especially in the South, the new county's area was not very different from the old geographical one.

Moreover the county boroughs, formerly the major reason for the geographical/administrative distinction, were now abolished. No city, however large, was to be entirely independent from a county. Places like Leeds, Bradford and Wakefield, though retaining great powers, were all to receive some services from 'West Yorkshire'. They were therefore 'in' it, in every sense. (Indeed, the type of county they were in — the 'metropolitan' type — consisted of nothing but such cities and their environs).

Small wonder, then, that Pears Encyclopaedia (Pelham Books, 1983) should summarise the situation thus: *Since the recent reorganisation of local government....the distinction between administrative and geographical counties no longer exists.*

So much for the prospects of the County of York. The new situation encouraged the new counties to adopt, not merely a political role, but also all the socio-cultural functions of a historic English county. Cleveland and Humberside were virtually invited to enter into jostling rivalry with the ancient county part of whose territory they had now come to occupy.

It is tempting to envisage more radical types of reform which might have avoided this outcome. Derek Senior's own proposal did not include counties at all, just 'regions', bearing the names of large towns, and 'districts', based on smaller ones. Cornwall's name, for instance, did not appear. Politically, its land was to be the concern of the Plymouth and Truro Districts within the Plymouth Region. Yorkshire's area would have been divided under cities like Leeds, Hull and York, at one level, and Pontefract and Scarborough at the other. Such a system could have left the historic county unchallenged outside local government for the non-political functions in which it used to be taken for granted.

You could say that traditional Yorkshire was now under pressure from an Act which in general paid too much regard to tradition.

Popular assumptions (i) — the distinction ignored. Whatever the Government's intentions, leaders of public opinion mostly assumed that the reforms went

44

beyond local government. In the politicians themselves such an attitude was automatic, and considering the amount of 'copy' derived daily from that particular source, it was perhaps inevitable that members of the press should hold the same view. Little attempt was made to distinguish place from politics.

Without moving an inch from their doorsteps, many Yorkshiremen may soon find themselves exiled from their home county.....Yorkshiremen Act Now....The Ridings will be swept away. Thousands of broad acres will be plundered to form local government areas with mumbo-jumbo names like Teesside and Humberside......I challenge Yorkshire's MPs: for once vote not for the party but for Yorkshire. Who stands for Yorkshire? (The question was asked by the Yorkshire Post, a newspaper whose very existence — and circulation area — symbolises the Yorkshire that lies outside local government). The appeal fell on deaf ears; apathy, not confidence in the county's survival, seemed the likely explanation. One peeress cared, without knowing what to do. *Lady Bacon weeps for torn county* ran the headline. *Her county of Yorkshire was "completely mutilated"..."I could almost weep for what has happened." Yorkshire and Lancashire became almost unrecognisable. Some villages even became part of Lancashire and some, part of Greater Manchester. "I do not know which is worse".*

The reaction of ordinary folk was mostly confused and indignant — those few, that is, who knew what was going on (if only because the press were asking them questions about it). But it bore out what Senior had alleged: it was place, their place and themselves, not politics, that interested them. *I shall always consider myself a Yorkshireman,* said the Sedbergh butcher. The Earby woman complained: *As far as I am concerned, I don't want to go in* (i.e. to 'Lancashire'). *I was born a Yorkshire girl and I would rather stay a Yorkshire woman. Once you are a Yorkshireman you stay one,* said the Whitby potato merchant. *I was born here and becoming part of an area called Teesside will not make much difference.*

There is some feeling for a distinction here, and in two other quotes, both from Humberside: *I'm all for it. I don't see why we should feel any loss of identity. We shall still be Lincolnshire folk and I think this merger is the finest thing that could happen to us all* (A draper's wife from Grimsby). A Hull man reflected the isolation of his city: *It has been drummed into us for so long that we are geographically cut off in Hull that I think the Humberside idea is a good thing. I shall always feel myself a Yorkshireman, whatever the name.*

But though such statements distinguish personal identity from political county, they do not suggest any expectation that more than one kind of county would have public recognition: one name, and one map — the new variety — is the clear assumption. Nor do they look far ahead. *Once you are a Yorkshireman you stay one:* but what about the unborn? A member of the Society for Yorkshire[12] worried about them. She dreaded the prospect, in years ahead, of having to say to her grandchildren: *This was Yorkshire, the largest county in Britain, taken away from us in 1974 just for administrative convenience,* and her answer, like that of her Society, was to fight the proposals, for she assumed, like the politicians and the press, that everything must be at stake in a political reform.

Popular assumptions (ii) — the distinction affirmed. Others were sure this was

45

not so. They depended partly on 'gut' feeling about Yorkshire's permanence, partly on an optimistic kind of reasoning about the future behaviour of non-political agencies: were not the Post Office interested primarily in where people lived? Why should they change addresses in Yorkshire, any more than they had in Middlesex? The concern of the map-makers was surely geography, not politics. Even more so, the tourist trade. If you still wanted people to visit Bridlington and Cleethorpes, why suggest they were no longer situated where they had been? Would not the weather-forecasters stick to real geography? Why should they assume in their listeners a knowledge of local government? The same applied to schools and textbooks. Probably there would be two kinds of map — the familiar one, and a more specialised one for lessons on politics. There would be no need to rename any part of Yorkshire for general teaching purposes.

Such were the thoughts reconciling traditionalists to political change. Where protest did occur — in Whitby, Great Ayton and elsewhere — it was because people put no trust in such consolatory assumptions. Their judgement was to be proved right. For the Post Office did change the Yorkshire addresses, the Ordnance Survey altered 'East Riding' to 'Humberside' on the only maps it produced, holiday-makers were invited to 'Tyne-and-Wear', and rain was forecast for 'Cumbria'. Most seriously of all, textbooks and teaching began to be changed. Wilberforce, from Hull, like Marvell the poet, was now represented as a Humberside man. Politics had taken over, not just geography, but history as well.

The distinction as an article of faith. It was in response to these developments that the Yorkshire Ridings Society produced, later on, a pamphlet containing its version of the situation. It is credo and catechism combined; and if its assertions recall, for some, the instruction given by Canute to an inexorable tide, it is only fair to acknowledge that it expressed many people's feelings exactly, and still does.

Along with a simple outline map of Yorkshire and the Ridings, the cover bears a challenge which combines jauntiness with the authentic dash of truculence: YORKSHIRE : HAVE YOU GOT IT RIGHT? Inside, we read:

The Facts about Yorkshire

1. Yorkshire by definition consists of the East Riding, the North Riding and the West Riding. This was how Yorkshire was created, by the Danes, in the 9th Century.
2. Over the next 1000 years Yorkshire and its Ridings developed its own geographical status quite separate from any other considerations.
3. In the latter half of the 19th Century an Act of Parliament set up county councils to administer Yorkshire. The boundaries of these council areas coincided with those of the Ridings and so they took their names and became the East, North and West Riding County Councils. Before this time councils as we know them did not exist.
4. In 1974 these councils were abolished and replaced by new ones whose bound-

aries did not coincide with those of Yorkshire. Consequently they were given new names i.e. Cleveland, Humberside, North Yorkshire, South Yorkshire and West Yorkshire County Councils. This in no way affected the existence of Yorkshire and its Ridings which pre-date county councils by about 1000 years.

There is some tension in the argument here — an emphasis on 'councils', rather than 'counties'. The word 'areas', however, does occur once. It was, after all, new areas[13], not just new councils, that were introduced in 1974, and the areas were called counties. But the Society recognises this in the first item of its 'Yorkshire Code' in the same document. *Always remember there are now two types of county, the geographical county of Yorkshire and the administrative counties*[14] *set up in 1974. Each type is separate from the other, both in area and nature.*

Two kinds of place? In the 1980s the media often tell us that the Selby coalfield is in 'North Yorkshire'. And so it is. But Yorkshire has its own geography; and Selby is not in north (or northern) Yorkshire:[15] more accurately, it is in south (not South) Yorkshire. The Notts border is little more than 20 miles away — the Tees, and even Cleveland County, more like 50.

But the two kinds of geography — administrative and 'real' — are often clearer in more urban contexts. The real Manchester is neither of the 'Manchesters' of local government — neither the Manchester District, an elongated rectangle sandwiched between two equally artificial creations, 'Trafford' and 'Tameside', nor the Greater Manchester County which includes distinct (and ancient) towns. For the city people mean when they use the word includes United's ground at Old Trafford just as surely as it excludes Rochdale and Bolton. With Leeds, things are different. The local government district of that name covers ground well outside the urban centre to which the name ordinarily applies. It would be misleading — and probably courting trouble — to tell the people of Otley and Wetherby that they lived in Leeds.

Imperialism. It must be acknowledged that local authorities themselves have not helped those wishing to distinguish place from politics. There is at work a kind of latter-day 'lebensraum' mentality leading to the strewing of waysides with the labels of power.

The people of Whitby, as we shall see, fought hard to escape from 'Teesside' (Cleveland) (Map 10 see Chap. 7) only to have their identity threatened from another direction. They used, after all, to have their own council, with the powers of an Urban District. Now, the most 'local' organ of local government is a council meeting 20 miles away; and when they return home from Middlesbrough across the high moorland by Scaling Dam the town they are approaching is indeed Whitby. Scarborough is 30 miles off. But the only sign on view reads 'Borough of Scarborough'.

As the motorist descends into the Wharfedale village of Addingham *en route* from the market town of Skipton — both of these being thoroughly good places in their own right — he is confronted with a sign bearing the legend: 'City of Bradford Metropolitan Council — Addingham'. It must surely be obvious that, of these six words, only one, the last, is necessary. For the ordinary driver

47

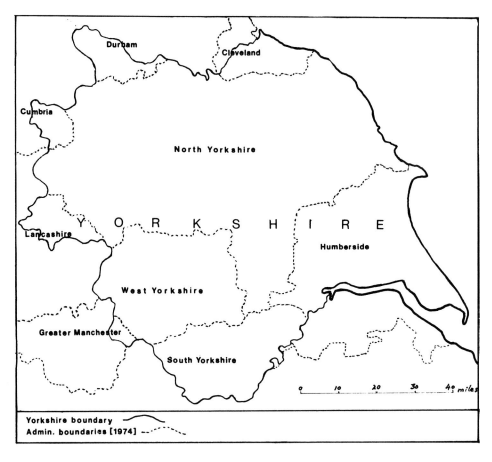

Map 2. Yorkshire: Local government, post 1974.

Map 3. Administrative geography: the "Manchesters", post 1974.

48

passing that sign is not usually meditating such questions as 'Under whose auspices is the refuse collected round here?', nor even 'Which authority runs the schools?' He wants to know where he is, if he doesn't know already. And the City of Bradford is not where the traveller is, at that particular spot. That great and important place is some 17 miles away by road. A sign with the word Bradford on it is required, not in Addingham, but where the town of Shipley ends and the city itself begins.

At the entrance to the village of Stamford Bridge, near York, there is a scene more perplexing than that which greets the visitor to Addingham. Three signs compete for attention. Two bear the village's name, along with, respectively, 'County of Humberside' and 'Borough of East Yorkshire'. The third states proudly 'East Riding of Yorkshire'. The claims of these rival notices is the general subject of this chapter and, indirectly, of the whole book. Here it is sufficient only to assert the prior importance of the village itself. Its name is Stamford Bridge.

These examples have, of course, different implications. At Addingham, though the name of a distant city obtrudes, it is really that of the Council. At Stamford Bridge and on the Whitby road the signs offer a name for the area itself, the very land people live on, suggesting something for them to identify with. Such, at any rate, must have been the reasoning which led to the overturning of a new 'Lancashire' sign outside a West Craven town used to thinking itself Yorkshire. I do not suppose the vandal cared much about local government. He cared about himself, his name and that of the land he thought he came from.

Naming the land: local government in its place. I think of this when driving eastwards along M62 towards Hull, Goole, Beverley and Bridlington. I pass the sign 'County of Humberside' and remember those who have felt themselves challenged by it. New political geography is in competition with old social geography — and physical geography, we might wish to say, as we head towards the Yorkshire Wolds and the Yorkshire coast.

For a new concept to oust an old one it must represent something fundamental. I recall the services provided by local government, and some of those which are not. Under that sign schools are built and run; the planning and repair of roads goes on; police and fire services are provided; houses are built and rented out; deprived children, the old, the handicapped receive help; refuse disposal is organised and land use planned...and so on. A vitally important programme indeed. But covering nothing like the whole span of ordinary life. The list excludes food and clothing, drink, hospitals and doctors, the car I am driving and the fuel it uses, electricity and gas supplies, television, radio and the newspapers, national railways and air transport. When I write I am aware that what I write with and on owe nothing to local government. Granted that the organisation which provides many services in this area requires a name, like 'Humberside', should it take over the very landscape itself, the ground we tread, to the exclusion of the old? Many have thought not.

Politics endorsed. They must nevertheless reckon — no doubt to their surprise

49

One village:

a county (or two)

....a borough

....and a Riding.

— with other symbols whereby the new identities are fortified. For each new county — Humberside and Cleveland included — was given its coat of arms, its High Sheriff, its Lord Lieutenant. And, however mysterious their function, these were to prove more lasting later on, in the metropolitan counties, than the county council itself. From the start they seemed to confirm the infant concepts from outside local government; and they also conferred an aura of antiquity. For the offices of Sheriff and Lord Lieutenant are centuries-old, and so is the practice of heraldry. The Humberside coat of arms links past, present and future in a particularly clever way. It includes symbols of Yorkshire, the East Riding, Kingston-upon-Hull, the Humber, Lincolnshire etc. and with its motto 'United we flourish' it seems to say two things: that their past is Humberside's past, and that Humberside has taken them over, replaced them, superseded them, in order to provide a prosperous future. From now on, they live only in it.

FOOTNOTES

[1] Research Studies 9: Community Attitudes Survey. (Evidence to the Royal Commission).

[2] It has accuracy, however, to commend it, in its own terms.(See Chapter 9, 'Action').

[3] Plus, for centuries, a fourth, York and its Ainsty.

[4] This reference, and the preceding one of 1888, I owe to Fr Francis, Organiser of ROOTS.

[5] Indeed, since 1440 Hull had had the status of 'City and County'.

[6] It is gratifying to note that the abolition of slavery was accomplished by an 'MP for Yorkshire'.

[7] See, on this theme, J.T. Cliffe: "The Yorkshire Gentry" (Chap XI), Athlone Press, 1969.

[8] Y. Post, 4 July 1969.

[9] Report of the Royal Commission on Local Govt. 1966-69, Vol.ii, HMSO, 1969.

[10] Middlesbrough Evening Gazette: 'Cleveland County Supplement', 1.4.74.

[11] Only Cumberland, Huntingdon, Rutland, Westmorland, the Ridings and the 'Parts' of Lincolnshire disappeared from the familiar list.

[12] See Chap. 4.

[13] *'For the administration of local government....England shall be divided into local government areas to be known as counties'.* Local Govt. Act, 1972. Pt 1 § 1.

[14] The administrative/geographical distinction, though long-established usage, is rejected by some as implying that local government counties are not the geographical areas they patently are. Alternatives to 'geographical' like 'traditional' and 'historical' suggest 'former', and are unacceptable to many on that account. the ROOTS organisation employs the term 'territorial'.

[15] See that strange southward-pointing Selby salient (Map 2).

CHAPTER 4: PROTEST

No other part of England was as badly affected by these indefensible changes; and of a population of 4½ million souls, hardly a voice was raised in opposition. So much for that famous Yorkshire independence and outspokenness!

So wrote John Martin Robinson in 1986.[1] A natural enough charge which leading Yorkshiremen of former times — Salt, Kaye Rollit, Crossley, the Fairfax-Blakeboroughs, J. S. Fletcher and others — would surely have levelled at their successors if they could have seen today's map. Why was it allowed to happen? We have noted one reason: Parliament had claimed to be reorganising local government, and it simply hadn't been clear that non-political things were threatened. Yorkshire, mainly, was such a thing. But even if it had been clear there was another reason. Since Yorkshire as a whole had no political standing, there was no-one to speak up for it. Indeed there was no single influential body whose job it was to know what (or where) Yorkshire was. A 'Yorkshire County Council' would have been aware of every last acre, if only for its rateable value, but no such body existed. Instead, the land had been shared between sixteen major local authorities — the Riding County Councils being only three of them — and each had been preoccupied, not unnaturally, with its own fate, not Yorkshire's, at the time.

So in the main it was left to villages and towns on their own, if they felt under threat, to fend for themselves. At least each place knew whether it was in Yorkshire or not, and whether it cared. And, contrary to Robinson, as the Maud Report (1969) was followed by Labour's White Paper (1970) — and especially when the Tories' White Paper (Feb 1971) and Local Government Bill (Nov 1971) appeared — there was plenty of caring and plenty of fending in the various localities, though often with the identity issue concealed, or complicated, by others. It is that protest, indeed, which is our subject here.

It was a fragmented business: Yorkshire's cause as a whole was not taken up. Leadership was lacking. There was one honourable, if small-scale, exception.

The Society for Yorkshire

John Fisher of Leeds had more reason than most to see the threat posed by the White Papers. Separation — as it often does — had sharpened his view and deepened his feelings: *I didn't realise quite what Yorkshire meant to me until I went to teach in Canada for three years. There I had the sensation that we had got something they have not. Now, quite glibly, that heritage we have is going to be destroyed; people in Whitehall are just out of touch.*

He felt he had to act. First there was the 200 mile walk from the Palace of Westminster to York in the summer holidays of 1971 — photographs at the start, with Big Ben behind him — and towards the end when, with White Rose emblem on his vest, he was joined by a handful of sympathisers for the last leg. A Retford (Notts) landlord, himself a Yorkshireman, had given him free lodging for the night, but there was little support in Yorkshire itself.

It's a great pity so few realise what is happening. I watched a TV programme at the time the White Paper was published. They read out the news, played 'Ilkla Moor' as a sort of tribute to a passing age, and that was it. How could any self-respecting Yorkshireman stand for it?

He felt his walk — aimed at publicity — had been a failure. The Lord Mayor of York, out to welcome him 'home', disagreed: *Mr. Fisher has done a magnificent job in bringing attention to this question but I wish thousands had joined him.*

Fisher had learned not to look to MPs. *Yorkshire had its pudding and its county cricket team : what more did it want?* seemed to sum up their view. He would look instead to non-political people, the famous and the ordinary. There would have to be a Society for Yorkshire.

In the Spring of 1972 — already too late to affect the Bill[2] — the group's foundation appeared in the local press. Sportsmen, 'personalities', landed gentry were to be canvassed. 'Debrett' was combed for members of the peerage to fight the Bill in the Lords. Visits were planned to threatened areas like Sedbergh. A signature petition was drafted; and a talented member portrayed the impending doom with graphic clarity. Starting in Leeds and York, they hoped to spread to the whole of Yorkshire.

What were they aiming at? The preservation, in some way, of Yorkshire's outer boundaries, within which, they felt, any necessary reorganisation could reasonably be confined. Their membership card contrasted, in simple outline, present and proposed future. They believed in three things: (1) Yorkshire's coherence as a place. *The geographical unity of Yorkshire, with its river system, its hills, dales, moors and rich central farmland, has not been appreciated......it is proposed to give away 3 vast areas of land...to neighbouring counties or zones* (the word 'zones' deliberately suggests men with rulers drawing articificial lines across the face of nature); (2) the distinctiveness of Yorkshire people and their culture — *a feeling of oneness, or Yorkshireness if you like* said Fisher. *There is an affinity* ran the membership card, *between its farmers and factory workers, its teachers and textile tycoons....when you speak to any of them you are never the stranger you could be in another county;* (3) the bond between people and boundaries: they belonged together. *Unlike people from Birmingham or Liverpool, Yorkshire people associate with the whole area, which is not just an administrative region, but has a distinct sense of unity.*

'Oneness', 'affinity', 'associate with the whole area' — few of the great or ordinary Yorkshiremen of the 19th Century or the pre-war 20th would have disagreed with any of that. Fisher had every right to believe it. Later on did he feel, perhaps, that he had been dreaming, or that he had been betrayed? Depressed he must have been, so doubtful was he whether Yorkshire could survive the proposals.

The Press was not always helpful. Somewhat awkwardly perhaps, Fisher had likened the boundaries to the bottle that was needed to contain a spirit, the spirit called 'Yorkshireness'. By the time the newspaper got hold of this image, 'bottle' had become 'battle' — *You must have a battle for the Yorkshire spirit.* The point was lost and another — a spurious one — put in its place. For no more peacable soul exists than Fisher — for all the pugnacious reputation of his compatriots. (He had threatened to resign at the mere mention of unlawful action to promote the Society's ends).

More generally, the reporting of the case managed to trivialise it by its farcical tone: the movement, for instance, was not going to be: *a living caricature of bloody-minded Yorkshiremen full of chauvinistic bombast; no daubing of 'Yorkshire for Ever' on walls, no contempt for lah-di-dah Southerners or unspeakable Lancastrians.* Fisher was alleged to regret that so many were following the county motto too slavishly : *Hear all, see all, say nowt.*

But it was not mainly for lack of serious journalism that the Society for Yorkshire failed. Lack of time, lack of know-how, lack of support, but, above all, lack of a clear route to such a large objective — the preservation of traditional Yorkshire and the identity of its people — these were the causes. How does a small group of ordinary citizens set about that? — especially given the ambiguous scope of a 'local government' reform. It was an interesting paradox: a group without political aims defending a non-political concept from political change.

The North Riding

Kippers and Bells. No place feels so distinctive, so separate, as Whitby. The principal sights — the rivermouth and the church and abbey on the clifftop — proclaim a place apart, owing nothing to any other. Whitby's debt, they suggest, is to the sea, and to her own spiritual past. The town is, first, of itself, alone. Secondly, it is Yorkshire. What it is not, is Teesside, nor ever was. But this seemed to its citizens their likely destination as they contemplated the various Government reports. For these showed a map separating Whitby[3] from Scarborough and linking it to Redcar and Middlesbrough.

Whitby, the Maud Report (Vol.i. p.189) had said, *a place of distinctive character, is nearer and more accessible to Teesside than to any comparable centre; it is within the circulation area of the Middlesbrough Evening Gazette, and not of the evening papers published in Scarborough and York. Its employment links outside its immediate neighbourhood are mostly with Teesside; 1300 Whitby people worked outside the town in 1966, of whom 600 went to Teesside (including Guisborough) and 500 to the nearby Whitby and Pickering rural districts. We expect the Teesside links to increase.*

Not many places as small as Whitby got a paragraph to themselves in the Royal Commission's Report. Two things are noteworthy. The use of the word 'Teesside' led to the belief that that word, and not anything with 'Yorkshire' in it, would be the name of the new county based on Middlesbrough. Secondly, the Commission's new areas reflected what it called the 'socio-geographic facts of modern life' (See, for example, Report Vol.1, p.180). By this it clearly meant such things as transport, work-places, newspaper circulation. Economics was

Apathy and doom. One view of Yorkshire and the reforms.

Whitby: Abbey, church and harbour. Photo by courtesy of Cliff Megson.

the theme: psychology, on the whole, was not. But later on the 'socio-geographic facts' of Whitby life were found to include feelings — a sense of identity with Yorkshire. The reformers had not reckoned with anything so primitive, so irrational; yet when the ultimate decision came that factor was incomparably the most crucial element in it.

Economics versus psychology. 'Facts of modern life' sounds so practical, so sensible. The real question is assumed to be: what local government areas will best promote people's long-term well-being in economic terms? It seemed to some so self-evidently the right one to ask that they were driven to the point of exasperation when ordinary Whitby people appeared to be answering different ones — such as, Who am I? and Where do I live?

Very many people are signing the petition for entirely the wrong reasons. Some sign readily because, they say, "I want to remain a Yorkshireman". Others do so because, they say, "I do not want my rates doubled". The speaker was a Whitby Town Councillor and the petition was the 'Whitby for Yorkshire' petition. Perhaps for 'sensible', practical reasons, perhaps for fear of domination by Scarborough — the 'Yorkshire' alternative — a majority of that Council had consistently favoured Teesside. By contrast, the councillors for the country areas round Whitby were against; a poll of their electorate had revealed only 5 out of 1200 in favour. And when the 'Whitby for Yorkshire' campaign began it was in the Rural District Council's offices that it met.

65 people attended that night. Within a month the Yorkshire Evening Post could report: *A Whitehall Minister was presented with six pairs of Whitby oak-smoked kippers today (20 December 1971). With the kippers was a petition bearing the names of 13000 people* – a very high proportion of the adult population — *who do not want Whitby to be included with Teesside. The kippers and petition were taken to London by members of the Evergreen Concert Party and members of the town's civic society dressed as fisherwives...*Both Whitby Councils were represented, along with the Head of the Grammar School. Scarcely a month later the headlines rang out: 'Petition that changed a Minister's Mind'.....'Bells of Victory for Whitby Win'.

How had it happened, this reversal of a scheme favoured not only by the Royal Commission, but in the White Papers of successive Labour and Tory Governments? After all, the Yorkshire Post had not seemed to exaggerate the size of the challenge: the adversary was *'something called progress. And the task of those who hanker after staying in Yorkshire looks as hopeless as the one King Canute was persuaded to take on'.*

It was partly to do with having support from the right men in the right place, Marcus Fox especially, MP for Shipley, a member of the parliamentary committee which heard appeals. But the real hero was the looming figure of Yorkshire itself. It summed up the 'wrong reasons' for which people supported the petition:

What's that? Stop me being a Yorkshireman? They cannot take that away from me (Whitby lifeboat coxswain).

This is a Yorkshire port and as different from Teesside as Hong Kong is from New York (another lifeboatman).

Whitby has always been Yorkshire and wants to be left there (head of a fish business).

They are a close-knit community here and fanatically proud of being York-shiremen (an immigrant from Leeds).

I will die happy if I die in the North Riding (Urban District Councillor).

The underrating of historic county identity and the folly of failing to reassure people about it in some official way — where necessary separately from local politics — are persistent themes in this book. No more eloquent illustrations of the need could be imagined than these quotations.

A campaign song, written by a local novelist and sung to the tune of 'My Girl's a Yorkshire Girl' tells the same story. This is not about local government; those who sing it need fundamental guarantees before they will — or can — discuss that topic:

> *Whitby's a Yorkshire lass, Yorkshire through and through*
> *Whitby belongs to us, aye by gum and we'll fight for her.*
> *Hands off our Yorkshire lass! As long as the North Sea flows*
> *We'll all fight on, with a Yorkshire will, for Whitby our Yorkshire Rose.*

26th January 1972 was like VE Day. There was applause in the Rural District Chamber. The YEP was lyrical: *Yorkshire rejoices tonight....because it will not be stripped of one of the most glorious stretches of coast and country in Britain .....This cruel amputation...would have thrown a traditionally Yorkshire community...into virtually alien land....The bells of St. Mary's are to ring in Whitby's victory over Whitehall.* A term never used before or since — 'de-Yorkshiris-ation' — was used to denote the defeated enemy. The Rector spoke of 'tremendous relief': 'we are part of Yorkshire, whatever the planners say' (Map 10).

No one, meanwhile, questioned the assumption behind all this joy: that the only counties were political ones. How could they be expected to?

Just Impediment. Elsewhere the North Riding had mixed fortunes. A last-minute campaign in Guisborough, the ancient capital of old Cleveland, failed, despite over 7000 signatures by February 1972. In other places, such as Yarm and Loftus, people were later to complain that they had never had a voice in the matter at all. But the villagers of High and Low Worsall (Map 10) had a victory to celebrate — with cheese and wine — after 150 had attended a 'Stay in Yorkshire' meeting, 300 signatures had been gathered, and a telegram sent to the Queen.

Probably the finest-ever display of Yorkshire patriotism, however, took place at Great Ayton. Over 1000 of the 4000 people living there drove in a mile-long motorcade the 25 miles to the County HQ at Northallerton to present a petition to Tom Kitson, MP for Richmond. Every car carried a white rose emblem and was decorated with white roses. Most carried slogans — 'North Riding for ever — Teesside never' or 'Don't let them industrialise Captain Cook's county'. (He went to school in Great Ayton). The campaign was marked by astonishing energy: 300 at the initial meeting; 2800 signatures; a visit from Marcus Fox and parliamentary colleagues to hear — and see — the case.

The County of Herefordshire was moved to complain about Great Ayton: 'No one visited us', they said. 'We went where we were invited', was the chilling reply. Besides, was not Fox a Yorkshireman?

'The feeling in the village takes you back to the war when there was such unity here', said one villager. *We are Yorkshiremen and women and we want to stay in Yorkshire; in Teesside we would be neither nowt nor summat*, said another. (All this makes one feel for the people of Middlesbrough and Redcar still, no doubt — some of them — valuing their own Yorkshire credentials. In Great Ayton, 'Yorkshire' was identified with rural, non-industrial things. It had a strange ring, considering the county's character in other areas).

I love Great Ayton, a campaigner had said, *but I would leave it to stay out of Teesside.*

Fortunately this did not prove necessary. The struggle succeeded, a comparatively brief affair at the end of 1971, whose climax came in a telegram to the Minister. He had described the transfer of Ayton to Teesside as a marriage between town and country. The telegram ran: *You have published the banns of marriage between Great Ayton and Teesside but there is cause and just impediment why these two should not be joined together in matrimony. The bride is already married to Yorkshire and has no wish to be divorced.*

The West Riding

Different Water. In the far North-West of Yorkshire there occurred a unique event. Whereas the White Paper (1971) had left the small town of Sedbergh, with Garsdale and Dent, in a county whose name was likely to include the word 'Yorkshire' (North Yorkshire), the local Council, by the casting vote of its Chairman, actually resolved to be excluded. People alleged later that one of the Dent councillors had thought he was voting the other way. Be that as it may, the Council's request was granted and this tiny enclave of the West Riding has been outside political Yorkshire ever since.

Not that there was, or is, any lack of 'patriotism'. One outburst springs from press archives dating back to 1970, to Maud's proposal linking Sedbergh with Lancaster. *We are Yorkshiremen and we damned-well want to stay Yorkshiremen,* was the clear, if unsubtle, reaction of the Council's oldest member. His spirit was to re-emerge 15 years later in the Sedbergh and District Action Group for Yorkshire whose members claimed lack of consultation over the original 1974 transfer.

As for the patriotism of the Council itself, in 1971 it was a nostalgic, political affair which focussed on the West Riding County Council: *The great West Riding has been pruned and we have been cast off – we have been stuck on to a new authority[4] with which we have nothing in common. We do not even drink the same kind of water – theirs flows eastwards and ours to the west. A headquarters in Northallerton would be preposterous.*

Perhaps the speaker had forgotten that the West Riding's water flowed eastwards too, and that Wakefield, like Carlisle, was much further than Northallerton. No matter. Kendal, with its 'services', was far nearer than either. Sedbergh followed 'logic' and Westmorland into 'Cumbria' (Map 9 See Chap.7).

Sheep don't pay rates. Further south it was not Cumbria, but a new political Lancashire, of all things, which threatened Yorkshire places with absorption, places as symbolic, moreover, as the White Rose itself.

The idea of flags showing the Red Rose being planted on the summits of Ingleborough and Whernside....is unthinkable at the moment. Reorganisation will be a numbing sensation for those of us who love Craven and Yorkshire, and the squiggly black lines on the map which for many years have represented county boundaries.

It was the Editor of the Craven Herald in February 1971 showing that he, at any rate, knew which way the map-makers would react to reorganisation, even if others didn't: the only 'Yorkshire' would be the administrative one. His readers obviously shared that view: all the North Craven villages voted against the White Paper (and logic, and Lancaster) and for North Yorkshire (County No. 5) — Lawkland, Austwick, Clapham, Ingleton, Thornton and Burton-in-Lonsdale, and Bentham (Map 4). They knew they were not voting for wealth. Man, it was noted, was not particularly well-off in the area; nor was he the only, or the most numerous, animal around. As the Herald pointed out: *Sheep don't pay rates.* Patriotism, however, brushed such considerations aside. *Surely they realise that most of us were born and bred in Yorkshire, and to expect us to become Lancastrians is a bit thick,* was an Ingleton man's comment. And it was a North Cravener, clearly, who rejected the idea of transfer because he couldn't face the prospect of Lancashire's climate!

Ingleborough, of course, didn't have a vote. It didn't need one provided Clapham and Ingleton voted the right way, and they did. Nevertheless, for administration, the Yorkshire Rose now shares the summit of Whernside with whatever symbol 'Cumbria' lays claim to (as though Cumbria hadn't enough mountains of its own); and that, together with the fact that those two villages nearly went into 'Lancashire', is enough to turn the white flower paler still.

Marriage of convenience. In West Craven, Barnoldswick and Earby, small towns each with its own Council, now became part of Pendle District in a new Lancashire (Map 4).

As the sun sinks slowly in the west, we say farewell to Barnoldswick Urban District Council sighed the Craven Herald, as it reported a Buffet Dance where 'Ilkla Moor' had been sung and three cheers given for the White Rose. It was the eve of reorganisation:*This page ought to be bordered with a heavy black band, the newspaper's traditional sign of mourning and normally reserved for the death of a monarch. While geographically we remain part of the White Rose County, administratively we become Lancastrians from Monday .*

Thus spoke an optimist, before the Post Office and the map-makers had revealed their hands. That 'we' explains it. Jack Heald, the reporter, habitual wearer of a white rose tie, lived in threatened Earby, and had once done the time-honoured 'pregnancy dash' to be sure that his wife gave birth on Yorkshire soil. (They only just made it — place of birth, the car park of the Bull Hotel, Broughton, on the Lancashire-Skipton road. It was a boy too, but not, as it proved, a Yorkshire cricketer to be). Now he looked forward to the retention of a distinction, that between geography and politics.

It was going to be a desperately difficult distinction to maintain in that part of the world. For, though one or two small places had protested and 'escaped' from the transfer, the truth is that many people, unlike Jack Heald, did not even want to. West Craven's emblem, long before reorganisation, could properly have been a rose that was pink, not white. Economic ties were with Lancashire; by World War Two 90% of industry was cotton; shops carried Lancashire products; men watched Burnley Football Club; many of them came from Lancashire themselves.

So local councillors had been pragmatic, if regretful. One spoke of their bread being buttered on the Lancashire side — the western side of each slice presumably; another had a confession to make about the company he kept: *I view it* (the transfer) *with great distaste, even though some of my friends are Lancastrians.* A third was unsure just what his nationality would be after the change: he spoke of *some sort of sorrow in being converted from a Yorkshireman,* but then — three sentences later — *we shall still be Yorkshiremen.* It was a marriage of convenience. 'Conversion' would not be complete. *The White Rose,* said the Herald, *is going red at the edges.......*

Banished in Bowland. Before 1974 the administrative West Riding stretched to within 8 miles of the west coast. (Indeed, long ago, Domesday Book lists all Lancashire lands north of the Ribble under Yorkshire — Lancashire being a later, 12th Century creation). From Yorkshire land on Fair Snape Fell, the famous Tower of Blackpool could be seen, and so could Preston, seat of that County Council whose successor assumed control, after 1974, in Bowland.

It is a lovely land, Bowland, the wildness of bare fells contrasting with rich valley pastures. Especially delightful is the Hodder, whose course south of the fell land to its confluence with the Ribble marked for so long the boundary between political Lancashire and Yorkshire (Map 4). Not many people live there, and there are only small villages, not towns — Slaidburn, with its famous 'Hark to Bounty' Inn, Dunsop Bridge, at the entrance to the Trough, Whitewell, Newton, Bolton and the strikingly named Bashall Eaves. Its secrets are hid from thousands daily tearing north on the M6 or A65, bound for Scotland or the Lakes.

The community is close-knit: *If you kick one person in Bowland you're not sure how many will limp because they are all inter-related.* (This information came in a BBC interview about reorganisation). They were (are) proud of Yorkshire too. One newcomer was innocent enough to ask, in 1944, whether it wouldn't be better if they joined up with Lancashire: *(We were nearly sixty miles from Wakefield) There was an old farmer sat across the table from me – there were 15 of us on the old council* (Bowland Rural District) *– he jumped up (he was very broad spoken), he glared at me across the table: "What, give Lancashire 'owt – not on yer life; it'll be over my dead body!"*

Strangely, that same phrase was to reappear in another of the interviews, not this time coming from an 'uncultured' farmer. A school meals organiser, having found her weary way to the remote little school at Bashall Eaves, was perhaps mingling hope with prediction when she told the Headmistress: *"They'll soon be pushing you over into Lancashire". And I said "Over my dead body, they will".*

And she said, "Why not?" And I said "Why not? And you work for the West Riding? We consider we're Yorkshire people here...the Wars of the Roses are still going on...we want to stay Yorkshire people". And then, poignantly: *I never thought that suddenly it would happen, which of course it has.* And the result? *I cannot see any advantage...the library service certainly isn't as good...I suppose it's prejudice, perhaps. Put me down as prejudiced – a prejudiced Yorkshire woman.*

Elsewhere the changes brought confusion. The boundary withdrew east from Bowland to the village of Tosside where it ended up running, so to speak, down the main, indeed the only, street. In 'Lancashire' were the school, pub, garage, church, shop, chapel; in 'Yorkshire' the village institute, the (former) vicarage, the caravan site. People grew used to seeing double, however good their sight. Gangs from both counties cleared snow, two library vans visited, Yorkshire rubbish was put in one wagon, Lancashire in another, each having used precious petrol and tyre tread to reach the self-same remote place. Most sadly, depending on their side of the line, 10-year-olds went to comprehensive school at Settle, their friends, having spent another year in a class thus depleted, either to grammar or modern in Lancashire. Boundaries, of course, have to be somewhere, and Tosside is no metropolis, but....

Saddleworth goes West: Sadness at the Cloggers' Arms. Nearness to somewhere else can work both ways. At Barnoldswick it reconciled people to political Lancashire, but for the residents of the Urban District of Saddleworth (West Riding) the nearest place was precisely the one they didn't want to join. A group of hill-top villages — stone built, like Haworth and Heptonstall — Saddleworth looked down, in more ways than one, on redbrick Oldham with its huge cotton mills, four miles away. Disregard, indeed, was often mutual. *That self-opinionated land where they have lived on the cheap for years (and how it shows!)* was one of the Oldham Chronicle's descriptions of this Yorkshire outpost and its rural rates.

But for all its White Rose status it faced westwards. Huddersfield lies thirteen miles to the east, over high desolate moorland (Map 5). (How on earth did Saddleworth ever become Yorkshire in the first place?) The lie of the land takes you down to Oldham and Ashton. No wonder the reformers, whether Tory or Labour, had destined the place for 'Greater Manchester'.

That was even the policy of the local council itself before the residents put their spanner in the works. When I paid a visit sixteen years afterwards the first parked car I saw had a Yorkshire sticker on the rear window. Its owner spoke sadly of a referendum in 1970 whose results had been ignored. Oldham Reference Library retained the startling figures:

Preferred local authority	First choice vote
Ashton	1836 (21%)
Huddersfield (Yorks)	5962 (69%)
Oldham	890 (10%)

Map 4. Bowland and Craven (West and North).

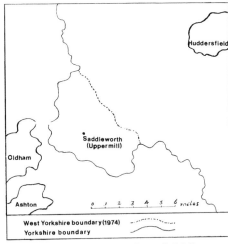

Map 5. Saddleworth and Oldham.

Built to last: in the Trough of Bowland.

Such was the verdict of sentiment. I read of a 'Save Saddleworth' campaign, of a parade of 350 marchers with placards and banners, accompanied by a pet lamb on a lead, and led by a brass band. Gardeners provided special displays of white roses. It was no use: 'commonsense' and those 10% had their way.

The Yorkshire Post aptly caught the mood of beleaguered Tykes used to disparaging the familiar but alien land they were now fated to join. Truculent, it was also bemused and half-apologetic — because in one way, their feelings seemed beside the point, and in another, local government, the cause of it all, did. *I can see why it's more convenient to go into Oldham – welfare services, buses and everything like that.... At the same time....we are accustomed to being Yorkshiremen. It is a sentimental thing.* The Post's tone reflected mingled pain and humour. One old patron of the Cloggers' Arms opined that in Lancashire they were different. They threw their money away, mostly on beer, while Yorkshiremen saved it. He said this, commented the Post, *taking an economical sip at his thrifty half pint.* But something serious was going on. Those votes for Huddersfield were not mere tokens. Sometimes our feelings run all the deeper for being irrational, not least when they are too irrational to be given full voice, even by Yorkshiremen.

Adieu, then, to Saddleworth — politically speaking at any rate — in the Yorkshire Post's own words: *Farewell: Jericho, Shiloh, Limbo, Blunder Ho and all the other improbably-named places sprinkled about the rugged scenery of Saddleworth, Oldham, Lancs (for postal purposes) or Saddleworth, West Riding (where the heart lies).*

The East Riding

That Bridge. In her published diaries Barbara Castle, then Minister of Transport, recalls the advice of a Ministry of Housing planner summoned to discuss a Humber Bridge on Sunday 16 January 1966: it should go ahead, he said, when a regional development plan for Humberside was agreed. The diary adds that the following day in a by-election speech at Hull she promised them the Bridge accordingly.

Doubtless the subject of Yorkshire identity was not raised during that winter weekend chat so briefly and blandly recorded. Yet many people in the East Riding were later to regard the arrival of the new county and/or its name as a personal blow; and many Yorkshiremen elsewhere have seen it as distorting, more than anything else does, the shape of the Yorkshire they value. The diary entries will interest those who see things that way, for they remind us of the history of that which alone made the new county possible — the building of the great bridge between Yorkshire and Lincolnshire. And they may reflect on the ironical fact that the writer was a Yorkshirewoman, born in Bradford, and that the Cabinet whose approval for the decision was no doubt needed, was headed by the Huddersfield-born Prime Minister, Harold Wilson. Not, needless to say, that the decision was in some way treacherous or even wrong: it only shows that things have unrelated consequences. In any case the principle of a Humber Bridge had been decided long before. (Mrs Castle's party, incidentally, won the by-election).

A Bolt from the (Tory) Blue. You cannot protest about something until you know what it is; and Humberside County appeared only at the very last minute. As late as the beginning of November, 1971, only eight months before the passing of the Local Government Act itself, the proposal was for two counties, one each side of the river. Then the news broke. County No. 8 — the north-bank county's reference in the DoE's Circular 8/71 — would be called neither 'Hullshire' nor 'East Yorkshire'. It would not even come into being. It had been superseded. The old barrier was now to be a bond — at least in theory. *Our proposals for these boundaries,* said Mr. Walker[5], the Minister, *resulted ...from their* (the local authorities') *failure to agree upon the basis of what they considered to be the right authority.* So 'Humberside' came to fill a vacuum. But there was another reason...*It was felt that the decision about the Humber Bridge meant that this area merited very careful consideration.*

Because of the vacuum, the Government had decided not to wait until the Bridge was built, as the Maud Report had recommended, before discussing the idea of a 'Humberside' county. The decision to build — finally announced by Labour in 1969 — was itself sufficient. They would discuss it now — indeed they would propose it now. No doubt they expected that the Bridge would have been in use many years before it actually proved to be — in 1981, seven years after the new county had started life. But whatever the timing, it could be taken for granted at some future date, as a means whereby car travel — especially that which involved members and officers of a County Council — between geographical Yorks and Lincs would be drastically shortened. In any case the process of 'very careful consideration' which was now undertaken was mostly reassuring. Labour Hull and Labour Grimsby, relishing their prospective partnership, sent a strong letter of endorsement, the local Liberal Association brushed aside questions of identity — *people should be prepared to move into the future without being tied by a desire to remain either Yorkshire Tykes or Lincolnshire Yellowbellies* – and even Beverley Rural District Council, though regretting the loss of 'East Yorkshire', gave its backing, relieved, no doubt, that the power of Hull was to be diluted in a larger Authority. 'Humberside' was home and dry.

'East Yorkshire'. But not quite. Harold Wilson once said that a week was a long time in politics. What, then, of two whole years in the life of Lord Halifax? In 1974 that bearer of a fine Yorkshire title was to become first Lord Lieutenant of the new County. Now, in 1972, as Chairman of the East Riding County Council, he despatched a telegram to Whitehall: *ERCC protest most strongly against the proposal for a Humberside County;* and Driffield Urban District Council, representing, no doubt, much rural opinion, congratulated him on the *firm stand to preserve the identity of the East Riding.*

The County Council decided on one last throw. Though desperately little time was available, within one month from the 'Humberside' announcement they had prepared a counter-proposal which, had it succeeded, would have spared many their crises of identity. It was based on the conviction that both the new counties, North Yorkshire and Humberside, which between them would obliterate the administrative East Riding, were larger than they should be, the former because it really was too big for efficiency — it is, in fact, the largest of

64

Which do you choose ?

I wish my home to be in

Tick to show your preference

A new **HUMBERSIDE** County ☐

A new **NORTH YORKSHIRE** County ☐

A new **EAST YORKSHIRE** County ☐

BLOCK CAPITALS PLEASE

NAME _____

ADDRESS _____

_____

Signature _____

(If you have any other preference state briefly)

I would prefer

_____

_____

_____

_____

_____

_____

_____

_____

Last throw for ERCC.

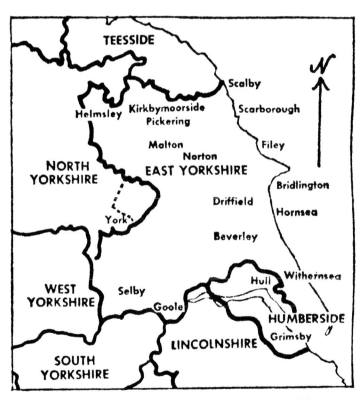

BOUNDARIES of the proposed new East Yorkshire and the more compact Humberside county.

Map 6. East Riding CC's counter-proposal.

65

the new counties of England in area[6] — and the latter because it belied the basic idea. 'Humberside' should be confined to the riverbanks, North Yorkshire should be smaller, and in between there should be an 'East Yorkshire' (Map 6).

Public opinion, moreover, would be ascertained. Somewhat controversially, £10,000 of ratepayers' money was assigned to the task, and by April 1972, an NOP Survey revealed 75% of electors favouring the 'East Yorkshire' proposal (and three-fifths caring 'very much' or 'quite a lot' which county they were in). The response to the Council's own questionnaire — ie those keen enough to reply, as distinct from NOP's random sample — showed 90% behind it, while in north Lincolnshire, Lindsey County Council's surveys were showing similar margins against absorption in 'Humberside'.

Help came from another quarter. The proud City of York announced its support for the East Yorkshire idea. Destined to lose its County Borough status whatever happened, and fated to be near the edge of North Yorkshire's 2 million acres, it would rather be on the edge of something much more compact, a county of which it was also more likely to be designated Capital.

Riding Low. But York's decision came in April 1972, only two months before the Act of Parliament itself, and by then it was all too late. There were recriminations. Bridlington, a town in which Yorkshire loyalty was never in doubt, lamented *the history of delay, indecision and inept action by the county council from the beginning of the present phase of local government reorganisation.* That was unfair: the Government had produced a last-minute card from up its sleeve and the flurry of reactions had had little time to succeed. What the episode, like the others, showed is that reform was a top-down business, paying little regard to popular feeling and even less to identity.

So the administrative County of York, East Riding, disappeared on 31 March 1974, and places as Yorkshire as Beverley, Flamborough and the Wolds came under a county authority whose title did not, and does not, include the old County's name. Did that mean that it had gone — from place and people — in spheres other than politics? Many watched to see what the response of opinion-formers in society at large might be.

FOOTNOTES

[1] In 'The Architecture of Northern England', Macmillan, 1986.

[2] But 2 whole years before the consequences of its implementation could be observed.

[3] See 'East Yorkshire' proposal: Map 6.

[4] i.e. North Yorkshire.

[5] On 16 Nov. 1971, during the Local Govt. Bill, second reading.

[6] The reforms were based first on city-regions, and 'North Yorkshire' simply gathered up all the mainly rural 'left-overs'. It was in order that it should not become even bigger still, that 'Humberside's' boundary was pushed further north than was strictly justified for a river-based idea. On such adventitious factors can new identities turn.

CHAPTER 5: BETRAYAL

The scales soon fell from men's eyes — and not just in Yorkshire. Three years before, the councillors of Wallingford, Berkshire, had consoled themselves, amid talk of old loyalties, with a familiar distinction: if their district *became part of a new administrative county of Oxfordshire it would also continue to be part of the geographical county of Berkshire*[1]. They did not discuss how that would work. In the event, on the first possible date, their local paper, the very one which had reported their deliberations, deserted 'geographical' Berkshire. 'North Berks Herald' became 'Abingdon Herald'.

If 'betrayal' seems too harsh a verdict on what is now to be related, that is certainly how it felt to some; and the 'culprits' included, not just bureaucracies, but flesh and blood. I visited Trevor Pearson, a Bridlington jeweller and tireless campaigner for Yorkshire. *Fancy ...., a Hull man born and bred, announcing on local radio, "this is a North Humbersider speaking"! A Humberside Cricket Club is being mooted in Hull. The death certificate now used by the Registrar states "born Humberside, died Humberside". I will not accept any such certificate for a member of my family.* He had a 'blazing row' with his father (a County Councillor) for addressing to him a postcard in the recommended, but much resented, manner. *I will close accounts with firms using that address.* The car outside his shop wore a sticker 'Yorkshire-born and proud of it'. *There is nothing I would not do to restore the name. If I could do that my life would be worthwhile.* He certainly tried hard enough. But first to those who caused his anguish.

The Post Office

County Councils feel remote but letters and postcards come right into our homes; and the county's name on the envelope is but an inch from our own. We all send mail; and for many, starting a letter is the only time we do something about our county's name. There at the letterhead, in telling people where we live and enabling them to respond, we actually write it.... whether with pride or indifference. Hence the power of the Post Office over perceived local identities. For in order to ensure efficient delivery it advises us how to address mail. In 1974 Parliament changed political Yorkshire. What would postal Yorkshire now look like?

Change. The answer came in a leaflet delivered through every letterbox in the land. It bore the coy title *A slight change of address,* the word 'slight' being at once an attempt to reassure and an acknowledgement that people might care.

In many parts of the county the changes made the word seem ironical. Until then, one word on its own, 'Yorkshire', had been sufficient, at the end of the address. Now it would no longer do. Where it survived you had to put something with it — 'North' or 'West' or 'South'. And in the East Riding the change could hardly have been more radical. 'Yorkshire' was replaced entirely — by 'Humberside', with the prefix 'North', in order to help, it was said, the sorters of mail. Patriots later rejoiced quietly to learn of the confusion arising from such 'help'.....letters destined for 'Bridlington, North Humberside' delivered to Bedlington, Northumberland; and another, with the same address, ending up on the south coast, where a resourceful sorter still knew where Bridlington was: 'not known in Brighton, try Yorkshire', was written across the envelope.

Response. That Post Office leaflet was probably, for many, the first they had heard about the local government reforms. It literally brought things home to them and some simply could not bear it. On the day the new order began the Head of an East Riding school changed the name of his house from 'West Keel' to 'East Riding'. *I was furious,* he said, *but when my wife said "change the name of the house" it was no sooner said than done. That symbolic act,* ran the Yorkshire Post account, *was the first ripple destined to blow up into a wave of resentment against the abolition of East Yorkshire in favour of North Humberside.*

Thousands ignored the leaflet and stuck to the old address. Businesses, being more concerned with 'efficiency' than feeling, mostly agreed to conform, and they provide over 70% of all mail. Yet four years on, the Post Office reported that one third of all mail was 'incorrectly addressed', the bulk of it, presumably, the 'fault' of private citizens.

Among the five new District Councils of North Humberside three kept 'Yorkshire' on their letterhead. At a meeting of Beverley District Council on 14 May 1974 it was... *Resolved: that the words 'North Humberside' be not used in the Council's postal address but the appropriate postal code, together with the words 'East Yorkshire'.* The voting, it is true, was only 23 — 19 in favour and some councillors described the move as variously 'irresponsible' and 'rather stupid'. One rejected what she saw as a *stand by hard-headed Yorkshiremen* saying she was *proud to belong to Humberside.* Another Beverley woman, however — a founding member of the Ridings Society — appealed to ordinary folk to 'stick to Yorkshire'. *Standing by her guns for East Yorkshire,* shouted the Beverley Guardian. *The patriots stand firm. We are happy and proud of being Yorkshiremen in rebellion.* Holderness was evidently undecided. An early letterhead, later to be altered, seems to have carried both 'East Yorkshire' and 'Humberside'. 'North Wolds' was content with 'Bridlington, East Yorkshire'.

In one respect, though, all three had it both ways. Their own printed mail invited replies to a 'Yorkshire' address. But they wrote to their ratepayers through the recommended ones.

Rationale. Why did the Post Office follow the local government reforms? It is a natural question considering the storm of protest which arose later on; natural, too, because before 1974 the county which had appeared in the recommended

68

addresses of Beverley, Bridlington and almost all the other towns and villages of Yorkshire had not been a local government county at all. Why change the principle now?

The first part of the answer is that it had the power to do as it liked. Though Government spokesmen had reassured enquirers that the 1972 Act itself did not affect addresses, the Environment Secretary could only reply later to protesters: *I realise how strongly feelings can be aroused on this issue, but decisions on postal addresses are operational matters which fall entirely within the responsibilities of the Post Office.*

'Operational matters'. The Post Office's task is the safe and speedy delivery of mail, not the reinforcement of personal identity. The addresses it deals with are 'postal' ones. Todmorden, well used to two identities long before 1974, would retain a 'Lancashire' address, for all its 'West Yorkshire' location. Even 'The Dalesman', an abiding symbol of Yorkshire life, had long received its mail at 'Clapham, via Lancaster', and would continue to do so now. The fact is, that 'Yorkshire' was a 'lousy' postal address — to quote a Post Office spokesman — because it covered so much territory and concealed the main sorting centre appropriate to each item. Any opportunity to split it into manageable areas seemed desirable.

Besides, at the consultative phase, few people had seemed to care. (If you only consult few people, of course, that is likely to be the result — over half a million people lived in the East Riding). Lord Peddie, Hull-born Chairman of the Post Office Users National Council, later revealed that from 50 businesses in the area only 5 replies had come, plus one from an MP and 3 from 5 local authorities. The Chamber of Commerce Bulletin, circulated to over 600 members, had produced two opinions, one for 'Humberside', the other for 'Yorkshire'. The Head Postmaster of Hull had advised that people in general would favour no change. In vain. Yorkshire was not to be exempted from the general policy for England and Wales.

But the decision rested on a more serious matter still, a unilateral assumption about the role of the new local government counties: *We were faced with a choice,* wrote the Post Office Chairman to Sir Paul Bryan, MP for Howden and a strong supporter of the East Yorkshire cause. *We could accept the new names and boundary changes – alternatively we could continue using the old names and boundaries, but this in turn would have been equally unacceptable to many people, especially the new county authorities. In addition, with the increasing use of the new names in the media, on maps and in schools, the old names were likely to become anachronistic........* Evidently Sir William Rylands foresaw little future for Yorkshire, especially in the East Riding.

The alternative. Pessimism about 'old' names, however, had not prevented the opposite decision being taken for Herefordshire and Worcestershire. The new county's name, 'Hereford and Worcester', was considered too confusing to be used in addresses. How could any town or city be said to be in another? — in two others? So the old names were retained, each for a separate postal county. Similarly 'Greater Manchester' was not adopted for postal purposes; so the citizens of places like Stockport (Cheshire) and Rochdale (Lancashire) continued to use in their letters the names of counties to which they did not pay rates. And in Scotland, that which in England was the exception was adopted as the rule: all the 'abolished' Scots counties — Banffshire, for example — were retained for addresses, in preference to newly-created Districts like 'Banff and Buchan' or Regions like 'Grampian'. And people were no less ready to accept the new administrative units just because they went on using the old names on envelopes. Quite the reverse. For one change at a time is enough; and the Scots, unlike many of the English, were spared the need to swallow two at once — both a new political system and the impression that they now lived in a different place.

As Sir William Rylands conceded, there had been no need to erase the word 'Yorkshire' from East Riding addresses. There would have been no inconsistency in residents of 'East Yorkshire' paying rates to Humberside County Council; if that had been the arrangement from the very start, it could have helped to give the new county readier acceptance. But once the opportunity had been missed, attempts later on to set the new address aside might well seem the first move in dismantling Humberside itself.

David and Goliath. The postman calls on most of us frequently enough, and our address is shown on every item of mail he delivers. It is, or should be, we feel, the place where we live. Colin Holt knew, and still knows, where he lives. The village of Fenwick is in Yorkshire. Not only that, it is in the West Riding. It is not in a place with a name invented for administrative purposes, 'South Yorkshire'. That phrase — if 'South' were spelt with a capital letter — should not be given any role outside local government. Even though it contains the most important word of all, accepting it would concede that the new areas were the real counties; it would betray those whom the new map had thrust into political areas not bearing the old name at all.

When Mr. Holt paid his Summer 1975 telephone bill he asked (respectfully) that next time the correct address be used : 'Fenwick, Doncaster, Yorkshire DN6 0EZ'. He repeated the process in the Autumn, but when the Winter bill arrived — again under 'South Yorkshire' — it was placed in his pending mail — his custom with three times wrongly-addressed items. The Post Office phoned promising to correct its error — but sent a receipt for payment which itself broke the promise. Subsequently all such items were returned unopened to York, Mr. Holt's telephone was cut off, and the world was denied its readiest form of contact with the Publicity Officer of the Yorkshire Ridings Society.

Years later, after privatisation of the service, 'Yorkshire' and Mr. Holt won. Phone bills were 'correctly' addressed; and there even followed a second victory, over another relentless sender of bills, the dreaded Barclaycard itself!

Unhappy endings. So much for one man's belated triumph. The story of conflict over the addresses of East Riding people is largely one of failure. A Post Office letter to Councillor Pearson in 1981 seemed finally to have closed the door. 'Humberside', after all, remained the name of the county, and 'North Humberside' the address of his part of it. The writer seemed to go to the heart of the matter: *The County of Humberside now clearly exists as more than an admin-*

70

istrative area and its identity will be reinforced by the opening of the Humber Bridge. Whilst I would be willing to meet you and other representatives, I must make it clear that the decision previously taken cannot be reversed.

Opposition to the new name had come to a head four years earlier. The 1972 Act had provided for local authorities to propose a change in their own names, if they wished, with effect from April 1978; and the East Yorkshire Action Group, led by Trevor Pearson, had proposed that 'East Yorkshire and North Lincolnshire' should replace 'Humberside'. But this, however accurate it might be, was so cumbersome that Government approval seemed unlikely even if the County Council could have been persuaded. Besides, its dual nature seemed to invite thoughts of partition one day, an outcome which most, though not all, councillors opposed. In short, it seems never to have been taken seriously.

Royal assent? Addresses were a different matter; and the adoption of 'East Yorkshire' and 'North Lincolnshire' as postal addresses was part of a petition to the County Council now mounted by campaigners north and south of the Humber. In a matter of months no fewer than 120,000 signatures were collected in the East Riding and 20,000 more by the North Lincolnshire Association. Gathering them took energy and courage. Trevor Pearson described himself as 'scared stiff of Hull', for the city was on the riverbank. Would it not support 'Humberside'? But into the pubs he would go and explain to the landlord why he was there. Then *Are there any Yorkshiremen here?* And eager signing would follow. Usually he was not back home until the small hours. Once, West Riding coach trippers to Hornsea made a detour to Bridlington to sign....only to be told that Humberside residents alone counted.

Certainly the affair drew media attention...and reached the most exalted ears. In a typical piece, on 1 Sept 1977, the Yorkshire Post, under the heading 'Yorkshire Protest: a massive outcry', reported Mr. Pearson as having written to the Queen for support....*Eventually I shall ask the Environment Minister to receive a delegation from East Yorkshire to present the petition. If he will not see us we shall take it to the Prime Minister.*

Some publicity was not exactly favourable. *I notice,* wrote one Hull Daily Mail reader (he was Lincolnshire-born) *that a large proportion of East Yorkshire supporters are senior citizens and I appreciate their desire to hold on to a valued past.......I admire their industry – particularly the elderly lady who talked my wife into signing on my behalf and was most indignant when I ran after her to cross it out.* For him, North Humberside — even the name, presumably — was *a great step forward out of Victorian times and attitudes.*

To his immense satisfaction, Mr. Pearson received a response from Her Majesty, then resident at Balmoral. Though it merely stated that the letter had been passed to the Secretary of State for Industry (!), its use of the address 'Bridlington, Yorkshire' looked like an endorsement of the cause from the highest possible source. There were many messages from humbler personages, not only in this country but in distant lands. *I would be delighted to live again in the East Riding, where I was born, instead of in a county with which I can find no ties or interest* wrote a Bridlingtonian from New Hebrides in the South Pacific. A Wiltshire vicar, not himself a Yorkshireman, offered sympathy : *I know how specially maddening it must be for a Yorkshireman to be told in a bossy way by the little grey men of the Post Office that there is no such place as Yorkshire any longer....I enclose extra stamps: you must be getting a lot of fan mail.* He was.

A resolution. However dubious some of the signatures, the County Council could not ignore a campaign supported on such a scale, though the misgivings of some members were obvious — and understandable, given that two of the Districts, Grimsby and North Wolds, not only wanted to change addresses but had asked the Government to split Humberside into two counties, one north, the other south of the river. So the resolution passed by the Council Meeting on 26 October 1977 was extremely cautious: *That this Council, in maintaining its belief in a united administrative County of Humberside, respects and supports the retention of traditional links by the use of the postal addresses "East Yorkshire" and "Lincolnshire".*

On the eve of the decision Trevor Pearson had been exultant: *I hope to be in Hull cheering our East Yorkshire heritage...We are Yorkshiremen through and through. I have been a Yorkshireman in exile ever since they created Humberside;* and John Townend, the Leader of the County Council, conceded that people *deeply resented the loss of the county name. Once the names East Yorkshire and Lincolnshire were restored a lot of the criticism of Humberside as an administrative county would cease.*

The situation did not justify such optimism. The resolution's bland words had changed nothing. How was the Council's 'respect' and 'support' to be translated into action? Would it change its own letterheads, for instance (as the City of Leeds was later to do), or its practice in addressing envelopes? Apparently not. The Post Office was simply told what had been resolved. Over twelve months were to elapse before the formal reply.

Wet Blanket. Throughout the campaign the Post Office's approach had generally been grudging, as a piece in the Yorkshire Post revealed: *By no means certain the PO will agree....A PO spokesman stated we must look at all the factors..careful study...detailed consultation with the people concerned* (all the people of the East Riding and North Lincs?) *....major business users will have to alter expensive computerised letterheads...PO must consider effect on own handling ...take some considerable time........*

Such wet blanket stuff presaged a dismal outcome. Optimists might draw comfort from reading (Yorks Post Dec.1977) that *the battle for the change of postal addresses....backed by huge public demand is to be taken up by Humberside County Council in the New Year* and that local MPs had agreed to raise the matter with the PO's Chairman; but it was not until June 1978 that news of the promised consultation came, and the terms in which it was couched could scarcely be described as neutral.

650 major businesses were asked for views. They were told that the original change had rested on consultation (but not how restricted that consultation had been or how pathetically small the response). And they were informed that: *In marketing and communications, in our experience, considerable importance is often placed on the corporate identity which an address like Humberside can*

TUESDAY EVENING, 27th NOVEMBER, 1984
Sale by Auction at 7.0 p.m.
at The White Horse Inn, Gilberdyke, of
A FREEHOLD FARM
"SALTMARSHE GRANGE,"
NEWPORT, N. HUMBERSIDE.

DRIFFIELD MACHINERY SALE

East Yorkshire
TUESDAY, 27th NOVEMBER, 1984

169 ACRE
ARABLE/LIVESTOCK FARM
LITTLE PLOUGHLANDS FARM
PATRINGTON, NORTH HUMBERSIDE
Freehold with Vacant Possession.
TO BE SOLD IN 5 LOTS
on APRIL 14th, 1988.

FOR SALE BY PRIVATE TREATY
88 ACRE
ARABLE/STOCK FARM
MILLINGTON GRANGE FARM
EAST YORKSHIRE WOLDS
Freehold with Vacant Possession.

East Riding conformists and non-conformists.

YORKSHIRE
is our
Postal Address

Royal Mail Brief
Issued by the North Eastern Postal Board
Royal Mail House, 29 Wellington Street, LEEDS LS1 1DA   No 2

A QUESTION OF ADDRESS :

Why it's
Humberside

Loyal Mail Brief
Issued by the Yorkshire Ridings' Society
67 Beaver Road, Beverley, Yorkshire.

A QUESTION OF ADDRESS :

why it's
Yorkshire

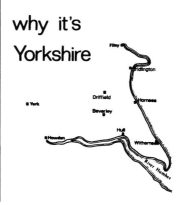

provide – and this is seen as an aid to attracting investment or business to a particular area.

A long way this, from the PO's proper theme of postal efficiency!! And it may have sounded strange to many firms which had long advertised goods through another name, one which for years had been commercially powerful, and was even the name of the TV channel for the whole region.

Meanwhile, one such product, the Yorkshire Post, had no doubt which way the decision should go. *The East Riding existed well before the Norman Conquest. When Roland Hill established the postal service in 1840 he found it quite expedient to use the place names which had served for a millenium in order to direct letters to their recipients.......The feeling of belonging to a place is a very strong one.... It is right that this mistake should be put right as soon as possible.*

"Heads, I win......". Despite such influential support, traditionalists feared lest the world of commerce should follow the Post Office's clear lead. *I hope business people will consider the moral aspect,* wrote one. *There are some things you just cannot put a value on, and this is one of them, a real, long-established county name replaced by a paper one.* He need not have worried. Two-thirds of the companies(434) replied, and almost three-quarters of them (298) favoured 'East Yorkshire', expense notwithstanding, while less than one-quarter (97) wanted 'Humberside'. So businessmen had now united with the people of the East Riding and North Lincolnshire, together with their duly-elected county council, in support of the kind of arrangement which the Post Office had itself initiated elsewhere...... and the answer was still 'No'!

Post Script. Before the reforms Government spokesmen had stated that the survival of traditional names for non-statutory purposes would depend on the people. So much for that. The Chairman of the North Lincolnshire Association was moved to write to his members about totalitarianism and the predictions of George Orwell regarding thought control. In response to the Post Office's leaflet *Royal Mail: Why it's Humberside,* which purported to explain the decision, the Ridings Society produced, and distributed widely, a pamphlet of its own, *Loyal Mail: Why it's Yorkshire,* to encourage supporters to stick to the old address. Members even handed one, along with a bunch of white roses, to the PO Chairman on his visit to Hull, and received, in return, a telegram of thanks.....for the flowers. The PO, incidentally, used arguments about the status of Humberside which could have been used to avoid the process of consultation altogether since they had been true for some time: the county had been created by Act of Parliament, it had a Lord Lieutenant, and its name appeared on Ordnance Survey maps, on signs at its boundaries and generally in the media. All these things, however, were equally true of the County of Greater Manchester where the Post Office had retained 'Lancashire' and 'Cheshire', and only the last — if that — was true of Middlesex, which remained, nevertheless, an approved address.

The Map-Makers

In everyday life addresses can reinforce the idea of a place, but for authentic facts about places — their names and where they are — we turn to maps. And since 1974, if it is Yorkshire we are looking for — 'Yorkshire' pure and simple — we turn in vain. Traditionalists had hoped it would be otherwise, but they might have known better. The example of Middlesex should have warned them. Certainly it was perplexing for even the PO had endorsed Middlesex. *The postal address of Teddington is still Middlesex,* wrote a correspondent to the Daily Telegraph (April 1981).......*An American relative who visited us recently was puzzled because he could not find Middlesex anywhere on a map of the United Kingdom. Surely a good cause for discontent?*

Ordnance Survey, the Government's official provider of maps, confirmed in correspondence with me that since 1974 it had had no choice but to omit Yorkshire from them. I had asked whether the Local Government Act 1972, by introducing *for the administration of local government......local government areas to be known as counties* had made it inevitable that, for instance, 'Yorkshire' must be replaced by 'Humberside' in the south eastern part of the county on all maps, whether 'political' or not. The answer was 'yes': the Ordnance Survey Act 1841 had directed the OS to ascertain and mark out the various boundaries in England, Scotland and Wales; and two Acts had since confirmed that duty — the Local Government Acts of 1972 and 1973; it was the names and areas laid down in those Acts which had to be shown.

The only maps, according to this, were now political. Hence the problem with Middlesex, banished from local government in 1965. And in Yorkshire the tables had evidently been turned by a strange sleight of thought: that ancient and unchanging place from which three of the new administrative counties drew their names, was now, paradoxically, beholden to them for its only appearances on maps and atlases. It could not look to Ordnance Survey to show it as something greater, to confirm its real extent.

But still a mystery remained. Yorkshire had never been a local government county. By what right, then, had it been shown on pre-1974 maps? The answer was something of a surprise. In that period OS had had to use its own definition of a county since, it claimed, *no reference to a definition of a geographical county in the statutes could be found.* It could not use the local government areas, complicated as these were by the existence of county boroughs. Instead, for each county, it had used the area of jurisdiction of the Lord Lieutenant. Thus the counties of maps had been, not political, but judicial. But even here Yorkshire had been characteristically awkward. Since it had no single Lord Lieutenant (each Riding had one) the OS had defined it as the area covered by its High Sheriff. A strange thing indeed that the old County, our familiar place, should have owed its position on maps to the work of a mysterious officer of whose functions — of whose existence — most people were quite unaware.

Early in 1987 appeared a gleam of hope. Bartholomews, the Edinburgh cartographers, reported: *the portrayal of the "historic" or "geographical" counties as opposed to the present administrative divisions of Britain is currently being reconsidered here.* They added that *it does certainly seem reasonable to show at*

75

least the major ones on maps where they differ greatly from political divisions. I had pointed out that Bartholomews themselves, in their 'Times Atlas of the World' showed, on the map of France, the names of traditional provinces, like Aquitaine and Normandy, which had lost their political status 200 years ago. Was not the omission of important, non-political, concepts from British maps inconsistent with this? I was to learn later that the result of the review was 'no change'. The reasons may be deduced from a holding letter to me: *cartographic design, available space, difficult to indicate the extent of the traditional Yorkshire clearly on small-scale maps, the fact that France is evenly covered with such geographical divisions, unlike Britain....* At least they were not claiming that Yorkshire had ceased, with its High Sheriff, to exist.

Boundary Commission: Parliamentary Matters.

Yorkshire and Westminster. Most of us are unaware of the extent of the constituency of the MP who represents us. Even so, it is a geographical area with a name, linking people with each other — party workers and voters. For some years after 1974 Yorkshire places now in 'Lancashire', 'Greater Manchester' and 'Cleveland' kept political links with Yorkshire because they continued to vote for Yorkshire MPs. Would they be allowed to go on doing so?

For the people of Earby, for instance, their home town was still, in 1978, in Yorkshire to the extent that they joined in electing the Skipton MP. Its future depended on the forthcoming review by the Boundary Commission...........and by 1980 they had placed Earby in the 'Pendle', Lancashire, constituency.

It was the same story throughout the land. Nowhere was a parliamentary unit allowed to straddle a new county border. Round the edges of 'Humberside', 'North Yorkshire' and the others the 'Westminster' boundary now followed the local government one — and reinforced it.

Defenders of Yorkshire greeted these developments with dismay. Old identities were being flouted. *Saddleworth Sad Again* shouted the Ridings Society's newspaper as it announced the proposal to 'rip' the place *out of its present Yorkshire seat (Colne Valley) and submerge it in Greater Manchester.* And the long-standing MP for the area was also, predictably, worried: *The people of Saddleworth say they are obliged to pay their rates and perform certain other chores for Manchester and Oldham but when it comes to the important things ....they are certainly Yorkshire supporters.* Another opponent sought consolation in the nature of the inhabitants: *If you can find a Yorkshireman's purse you may be able to steal it* — another reference to rates? — *and you may be able to push him out of the county, but you will never make him anything else but a Yorkshireman.*

Vainly did the Ridings Society strive at the public enquiry to retain constituencies consistent with traditional Yorkshire — 'Cleveland and Whitby' — for instance, lying wholly within the North Riding but crossing the North Yorkshire/Cleveland boundary. Its proposals, set out in White Rose Paper No.3: 'Knowing where to draw the line' (1980), were all rejected by the Commission. Indeed the Society found later that statutes under which the Boundary Commission was working (Acts of 1949 and 1958) ruled out the crossing of local government boundaries by parliamentary ones.

Yorkshire and Strasbourg. Already electoral units of a new kind altogether had been proposed. However lukewarm British people had been towards membership of the EEC, Europe seemed likely to become more and more influential in UK affairs. In future decades and centuries would Yorkshire people be able to vote together in areas which made sense of their past? The Ridings Society felt sure that they should; and in White Rose Paper No.2 (1978) it listed seven constituencies: East Riding with York; North Riding; and the West Riding divided into five parts (Map 7a). Apart from the North Riding's great size these ideas mostly had compactness as well as a sense of tradition to commend them compared with those of the Commissioners which predictably included 'Cleveland' and 'Humberside'.

But their consultative proposals of 1978 at least offered a glimmer of hope, for they were based on Westminster constituencies which had not yet been revised; and some of the areas were inconsistent with the new local government — Grimsby ('Humberside') being shown in a 'Lincolnshire' constituency, Goole ('Humberside') in one called 'Yorkshire, Central'. But by the time consultation was over, in January 1984, the Westminster pattern had been changed and 'Europe' was seen to be lined up with it. Grimsby was in 'Humberside'. Goole, it is true, was not, but neither was it in something called 'Yorkshire'. 'Yorkshire, Central' was now, simply, 'York', a mammoth area linking the Isle of Axholme with Staithes, north of Whitby, 80 miles distant. The Ridings, of course, were to have no role.

'Yorkshire in Europe' presents, indeed, a strange picture — two constituencies, 'York' and 'Cleveland and Yorkshire North', especially (Map 7b). Simply because 'Cleveland' on its own does not have 500,000 voters, two Westminster constituencies to the south are added to it; and the resulting links are remarkable: the people of Skipton, an inland market town in a rural setting, are invited to vote with those of the Hartlepools, 75 miles away on the Durham (Cleveland) coast. It is no disrespect to the inhabitants of either place to question whether many of them know where the other one is. But then, instead of channelling loyalties, the Boundary Commission had had to apply a formula to England — as a baker takes a biscuit mould to the pastry. The enterprise concerned — the EEC — was controversial enough. Rational boundaries and sympathetic names might just have helped.

Offences to Old and Young

But electoral boundaries are a long way from most people's feelings about Yorkshire. It wasn't so much these that made them feel betrayed. It was the apparently ceaseless references to new names in the local and national media, especially 'Humberside'. The name of the County Council naturally occurred often in reports of its business; a local radio station itself bore the name; guidebooks and textbooks fell into line. *Have you seen any of the new local history books?* asked one old campaigner. *No trace of East Yorkshire. In fact I*

77

Map 7a. Yorkshire for Europe – YRS proposals, 1978.

North Riding

West Riding 1

WR 2

East Riding + York

WR 3

WR 4

WR 5

1 Bradford and Dales
2 Leeds
3 Halifax Huddersfield Wakefield
4 Barnsley Doncaster Goole
5 Sheffield and Rotherham

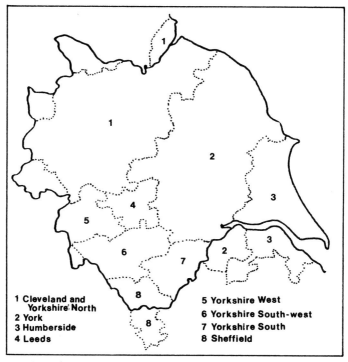

1 Cleveland and
   Yorkshire North
2 York
3 Humberside
4 Leeds
5 Yorkshire West
6 Yorkshire South-west
7 Yorkshire South
8 Sheffield

Map 7b. Against the grain: EEC constituencies, 1984.

was reading a book about the Second World War and even it (published 1976) referred to the Humberside area. Worse still, the word began to be used of the area's inhabitants: 'Humbersiders — Plan-deciders' ran a consultative document from the County Planning Department, shoved through every letterbox. A 76 year-old complained of 'constant propaganda' and feared that it was succeeding: radio listeners were constantly referred to as 'Humbersiders', were asked to display car stickers with the name and to sell T-shirts and souvenirs. There were, of course, some who did not mind, and one of them poured scorn on one who did, though the extreme antiquity of his examples made his weapon two-edged: *He should have marshalled his Yorkist battalions before now.....what about Brigantes, Deira or even Northumbria, all previous names for his East Riding of Yorkshire? The next thing he will want is the wolves brought back to roam the Thwing countryside.* Yorkshire patriots could never now see 'Humberside' as a mere term of geographical reference within Yorkshire, meaning the riverbank area, the sense in which it had been widely used long before 1974. For them it clearly meant the renaming of part of Yorkshire — a part, indeed, which must exclude the old county. And every instance of that improbable duo, 'Yorkshire and Humberside', seemed to confirm this. In desperation, and with the utmost seriousness, a Hull pensioner applied to the Home Secretary for *naturalisation papers for Yorkshire...*only to be told that such procedures involved separate nationalities and that the Home Office had no power to create a new one within the UK. Anguish of a similar kind is evident in the outpourings of another senior citizen: This was not what he had risked his life in war for: *It seems that this country is run by bureaucrats – dictators; the name 'North Humberside' is an insult; after all it's people that count – they are supposed to help us and give us what we want.* A dialect poet took refuge in the unchanging geography of the mind:

> *Fresh lines on't map or new address means nowt;*
> *Thoo still can dwell iv this here spot sa fair.*
> *Name's nobbut off – t'East Ridin nivver dees;*
> *Safe iv oor heearts it bides for ivver mair*[2].

So much for the older end. Neither did the young go unscathed, even the very young. One Ridings Society member reported, in 1979, his sense of shock at reading the new name entered on his son's birth certificate as the place of birth four years before — and as the birthplace of his wife. With much relief he was able to announce that the Registrar General in London had authorised the local Registrar to 'correct' the entry in the presence of witnesses. Inspired by such an example, the Society's Journal urged members to dedicate the International Year of the Child (1979) to the Yorkshire child in particular:

If we are not careful our children will be alienated from us. Already they speak of different measures for length, weight, volume, liquids and money; already they are being trained to be happy Humbersiders, contented Clevelanders and Cumbrians, lack-lustre Lancastrians and subservient South Yorkshiremen. Those little children who attend school for the first time this year will be told that the three Ridings of Yorkshire had ceased to exist by the time they were born......This sort of nonsense must be stopped.

FOOTNOTES

[1] North Berkshire Herald: 25.3.71.

[2] From 'East Riding': Kathleen Stark (Transactions of the Yorkshire Dialect Society).

CHAPTER 6: RESISTANCE

The introduction of a new county name into the life of the East Riding was not a sudden affair. Some months after reorganisation the old ones still seemed to flourish — in the columns of the Driffield Times, for instance. Published by 'East Yorkshire Newspapers' and printed by 'East Yorkshire Printers', it continued to feature an 'East Riding Top Ten' for 'pop' enthusiasts. A Motor Mart and an Auction and Property Market both carried the 'East Yorkshire' label in the December 1974 issues. The more observant of readers, however, might have noted with misgiving a change which occurred very early indeed in the new era. Under its front page title, the paper used proudly to display the words: 'Circulation guaranteed throughout the East Riding of Yorkshire'. By 16 May 1974 this claim was no more to be seen.

A month before, the same paper had carried a report which served both to encourage and dismay. A Beverley woman had written to the Prime Minister about Yorkshire on the anniversary of the granting of a charter to her home town; and the DoE's reply was reassuring: *There is no statutory reason why Yorkshire should not keep its present boundaries for sporting or other reasons as has Middlesex, which for local government is part of Greater London.*

Some did not welcome such news: *The Ministry decision,* said the paper, *has come as a surprise to Councillor Harry Lewis, Leader of Humberside County Council, who is to take the matter up with the Minister and a local MP. He said he knew many people had a sentimental attachment to Yorkshire but they now had new boundaries and a new county with which he wanted people to be identified: "We have applied for armorial bearings of our own and we would not have done that if we had not thought Humberside was real."*

In the same article the 'Times' reminded readers that the Post Office was to introduce the new address from 1 July, *although originally the Department said that the old addresses would be used.*

Battle joined: Yorkshire Ridings Society

Such portents, however confusing to others, sent a clear message to the small group who were now to found the Yorkshire Ridings Society. Unknown to each other, about a dozen people had, in the period leading up to the change, sought Government views about continuity — in maps, addresses and so on. It was now obvious that such assurances as they had received were likely to prove worthless. Unlike administrative Middlesex, the East Riding of local government had been replaced by something which — prompted by its county status — felt obliged to seek all the loyalties which the ancient territorial divisions of England had commanded for centuries. Yorkshire had a battle on its hands.

Aims. Certainty about the danger was matched by clarity about the issue. This was not local government, but identity. The Society founded in December 1974 did not seek to dismantle new political arrangements or even to rename new counties but merely to keep new local government names where they belonged — in local government. And though for obvious reasons its membership was disproportionately from the East Riding its brief covered all three and the City of York, the whole of the geographical county, for new names affected it all. In this respect it was the true successor to John Fisher's Society for Yorkshire — with one difference of emphasis. For him, the only boundaries that mattered were the outer ones of the whole county: for the Ridings Society, its belief that the *de facto* existence of Yorkshire for 1100 years implied a geographical status which could not be cancelled by the 1972 Act must apply equally to the Ridings which were just as ancient. Hence the Society's aims:

(1) To preserve Yorkshire and its Ridings intact as an integral part of the UK.
(2) To oppose all changes which endanger the achievement of item 1. For example: alteration of postal addresses, the removal of signs and symbols of Yorkshire and its Ridings, the redrawing of maps to the exclusion of Yorkshire and its Ridings.
(3) To present the views of the people of Yorkshire on the above matters, to the Government, the media and any other organisation or individual as necessary.
(4) To uphold and propagate the traditions, life-style and customs of Yorkshire.

The tone is one of self-assurance, notably at (3), where some — Councillor Lewis, for example — might challenge the representative function which the Society claims for itself. Nevertheless all lovers of Yorkshire — and of Huntingdon and Rutland, Somerset and Westmorland etc — and England — owe a debt to the Society for consistently and clearly upholding the distinction between place and politics over so many years.

A note on age. Loyalty to Yorkshire is often assumed to be characteristic of advancing years, a condition which encourages, it is felt, a tendency to cling to the past. It can therefore be disregarded as 'sentimental' — a word in frequent use — something that the lapse of time will bring to an end in the most natural way of all.

So it is worth noting that, of the ten members of the Founding Committee of the Yorkshire Ridings Society, none was over 36 at the starting date and half were under 25. Nor could they be described as a bunch of academic dreamers, remote from the workaday world: besides three teachers, a businessman and a housewife, they included a farm labourer, a clerk, a machine operative, an electrician and a warehouseman/van driver.

Means to an end. From the start people turned to the Society as a refuge from a situation they could not accept, one whose dilemmas only the YRS sought to explain. The car stickers, T shirts, bookmarks, pens and pencils, key fobs, note paper, memo pads, franking marks ('Yorkshire our postal address'), lapel badges and posters — all with the County's name or a Riding's — allowed them to proclaim their identity, to themselves and to others. A Journal kept them in touch, publishing traditional recipes, announcing victories of old names over new, reporting conflicts with Post Office and Barclaycard. Members kept YRS diaries, referred to YRS calendars and were vigilant in scanning the media for items to report to colleagues: how 'Mastermind', the famous TV Quiz, having spoken of the Ridings as things of the past, had apologised on being corrected, and how Brian Rix, the Hull-born actor, had given the Society and the East Riding a 'plug' on the radio.

The Society has not been run as a 'movement', depending on ever-increasing membership. It has behaved more like a pressure group, defending its distinction through policy documents, letters and appearances on radio and TV. Even more characteristic is the kind of symbolic activity likely to gain media coverage — the Publicity Officer's stand against the Post Office, the planting of boundary signs on private land at the entry to the Ridings, the raising of the Yorkshire flag at the top of Sutton Bank on New Year's day — in a raging blizzard — to inaugurate the County's twelfth century. A 'Great Yorkshire Walk' was instituted, covering the longest possible diagonal (144 miles) from the Westmorland border, near Sedbergh, to Spurn Point, a seven-day tramp ending, again symbolically, on 1st August. There was a bouquet of white roses sent to the Queen *on behalf of the people of Yorkshire* on her Silver Jubilee, an action promptly acknowledged by the Palace in a letter addressed to Mr. Holt at 'Fenwick, West Riding of Yorkshire'.

Yorkshire Day. But, most successful of all, there is Yorkshire Day, 1st August, founded by the Society in 1975 and celebrated more widely with every succeeding year. It is the anniversary of the Battle of Minden (1759) when Yorkshire and Lancashire soldiery are said to have fought with distinction, and to have gathered and donned red and white roses to honour the fallen. Despite such origins it is not intended as a solemn memorial of things past — like Armistice Day — but as a triumphant celebration of something that has not died and never will. Its analogues are the national days of Scotland and Wales. It is a time for sporting a white rose, eating from a Yorkshire menu[1] (many restaurants and inns rise to the occasion) and going on a Yorkshire walk. A procession of civic dignitaries from all over the County took place for the first time in 1985, appropriately in York, along a route from the Mansion House to the Minster, where a service was held (see Chap. 8 'Yorkshire in Focus'). A well-known Leeds Brewery offered half-price beer in its pubs that night. So well-established, indeed, has the day become that it is evidently now seen by some as an ancient festival of mysterious origin. The soldiers sported roses in 1759, it is said, because it was Yorkshire Day...! Considering the Society's slender means, it is a considerable triumph.

Central to the Day is a ceremony whose location and use of languages symbolises the permanence of the County. It starts at a time which represents, in its numerical form (eg 11.11) the lapse of years between the year of Yorkshire's supposed founding, 876AD, and the current year. The place is York; and outside three of the ancient Bars and inside the fourth (Monk Bar) — that is to say, on ground belonging to each of the Ridings and to the City itself — a

'Declaration of Integrity' is read, in words suitably positive and defiant, not to say aggressive.

Your attention please! I, being (a native of and) resident in the East/North/West Riding of Yorkshire declare:
> *that Yorkshire is three Ridings and the City of York with these boundaries of .... years standing;*
> *that the address of all places in these Ridings is Yorkshire;*
> *that all persons born therein or resident therein and loyal to the Ridings are Yorkshire men and women;*
> *that any person or corporate body who knavishly ignores or denies the above shall be outcast and unfit for the company of civilised men and women.*
> *These declarations made this Yorkshire Day 198...*
> *YORKSHIRE FOR EVER! GOD SAVE THE QUEEN!*

Individuals are invited to make the Declaration themselves wherever they happen to be at the time of the official event and readings are reputed to have taken place even in foreign parts eg Saudi Arabia. But they are not expected to follow suit in the matter of languages; for at York each of three tongues is used, Old English, as well as the modern version, and Latin!

Lovers, of course, are noted for their excesses; and are wont to be excused them. The Society would spurn such patronising while acknowledging the feelings. For there is no doubt that we are in the presence of very deep ones. The bond between place and people, the nature of roots and identity, are the themes addressed. The linguistic formulae call to mind parliamentary, perhaps even religious, ceremonial. Local government, meanwhile, is nowhere to be seen.

YRS and politics. It is, of course, an article of faith that the real County has not been touched by administrative reforms, and this might be thought to imply indifference to politics. But the Society cannot ignore the buffeting which the notion of Yorkshire has been subject to since 1974. Indifference, therefore, is not the word. If it had been, there would have been no Society.

So there is, in the Journal's pages, satisfaction to be derived from public discontent with the new county councils, and forecasts of their imminent demise. There is ridicule of their attempts to create a past ('West Yorkshire Archaeological History'), a non-political present ('Humberside Show') or a tourist personality ('Visit South Yorkshire'). And there are the White Rose Papers, statements on public issues affecting Yorkshire. One of these, 'Painting the Clouds with Sunshine', reflects annoyance at meteorologists' tendency to refer to new counties in weather forecasts and offers the real Yorkshire as a standard 'soft-edge' weather region. The others deal with political matters like constituency boundaries and devolution. All take the same starting point, 'true Yorkshire'.

Counter-attack: East Yorkshire Action Group

Since none of the new Districts or Counties corresponds in area with Yorkshire and its Ridings, the Ridings Society cannot campaign to have them renamed.

That would put cart before horse, by acknowledging the heresy that the County is merely an amalgam of local authorities which happen to have the right word in their names. But there were some members and sympathisers — especially in the East Riding — for whom such purity of doctrine was not enough. Led by one who was a North Wolds councillor, they were inclined, perhaps for that reason, to take political names more seriously; and surrounded more and more by the new ones, they felt that the old needed all the help it could get — even from politics — if it was to survive for long anywhere but in their hearts. The word 'Action' in their chosen title summed up the mood. Chapter 5 related their efforts, ultimately fruitless, to replace 'Humberside' as the county's new name and as a recommended address.

Renaming the Districts. At District level they were to be more successful. Early in 1981 the Yorkshire Post reported that *the county name East Yorkshire* was to be *put back on the map* by three borough councils — North Wolds, Beverley and Holderness. These covered between them the vast bulk of East Riding ground, omitting only the area of the Hull district and part of Boothferry. North Wolds, the most northerly, made the first and boldest strike. Believing itself to have been saddled with *a geographically misleading misnomer* — someone commented that it had a ring of 'Dartmoor' — it had already tried, in 1978, to move to 'Bridlington and Yorkshire Wolds' but the Minister, whose approval was then needed, had objected. By now the rules allowed it to amend its own title; and it was not going to beat about the bush. The name that it chose was none other than 'East Yorkshire', leaving the other two councils to adopt the precious words as best they could. And they were not too pleased, for North Wolds was by no means the whole of East Yorkshire. In usurping the name they were *worse than jackals or hyenas*, claimed one Beverley councillor, though a colleague asked, more charitably, who could blame them *with a name like that.* For Beverley itself the Council proceeded to adopt, by a handsome majority, the title 'East Yorkshire Borough of Beverley'. It was assured that the move had the support of 2000 people (the work of the Action Group) and that *it was time to listen to the voice of the people. It will give people back that feeling of identity that was lost when Humberside was born.*

As for Holderness, its Council eventually rejected, by 16 votes to 11, the proposed title 'Borough of Holderness (East Yorkshire)'. Among the minority were some who had actually feared a drift of population to the newly-named 'East Yorkshire' if Holderness were not to change. Opponents felt the proposal might read as though Holderness were a mere part, or adjunct, of the new 'East Yorkshire'. One summed it all up in a manner which would have gladdened the Ridings Society: *There is no point in putting "East Yorkshire". Everyone knows Holderness is in Yorkshire*[2].

That was one approach to the issue, and if he was right, then political names didn't matter, and North Wolds had had no need to change. But it had, and there were problems, as one correspondent reminded Trevor Pearson, leader of the Action Group: *Good to hear of the new name of your District, but what about my use of Kingston-upon-Hull, East Yorkshire, as my address?*

At least, however, it was two Authorities, not one, which now bore an 'East

Yorkshire' label, a fact which served to disprove what some might otherwise have been tempted to assume — that the term was henceforth wholly restricted to one area. If two could use it, there was no reason why all five north of the river should not do so one day.

The Ridings Society, meanwhile, was unmoved. According to its Journal nothing had changed; no prefixes — whether North or West, South or East — and no new titles applied to local authorities, whether 'Cumbria', 'Cleveland', 'Humberside', 'Durham', 'Lancashire' — or even 'Yorkshire' — made a scrap of difference; this last name still adhered to the *place* it belonged to — and in the people's hearts, a fact which explained all the (unnecessary) preoccupation with political nomenclature.

Applause. Delight, however, was the response of Mr. Pearson's many far-flung admirers to the news about 'North Wolds' and Beverley:

> *Congratulations on UDI from Humberside* (Ashby-de-la-Zouch).
> *Thank you for brightening my day. When I opened the Telegraph* (ie the national Daily Telegraph) *and saw your article I cheered loudly in your support* (Worthing, Sussex).
> *I was blistering mad when the name 'Humberside' was suggested and nearly went beserk when it was to be officially recognised* (Hornsea-born surgeon, Welshpool).
> *Here we have to contend with the stupid 'Avon' business. I have always been surprised at the supine way Yorkshire folk took to the dismemberment of their county.*(Taunton).

A supporter in Middlesex wrote *as an exiled Yorkie who has the Free Press* (the Bridlington Weekly) *sent like a Red Cross parcel every week.* Greetings came from far and wide, from Weymouth, for example, Carlisle, Cockermouth, Eastbourne, Aberdeen....and Jeddah, Saudi Arabia. So celebrated a figure had Mr. Pearson become that an envelope with the mysterious address: Mr. EAST YORKSHIRE, CARROTS FOR CARATS, (An allusion to the jeweller's shop?) YORKSHIRE arrived only a week after posting — a tribute, no doubt, to his old adversary, the Post Office, as well as to his own fame.

The Case for Partition: North Lincolnshire Association

Strong resentment at the new county's name had long been felt south of the Humber. In April 1986 a correspondent to the Yorkshire Post wrote: *Who can doubt that any true Yellowbelly finds the term 'Humbersider' both alien and offensive?....On the south bank the electorate have to contend with this impediment in so many areas – cricket, nature conservation and tourism spring readily to mind. It has to be more than a mite ripe when the present leader of the county council...has had the temerity to try to form a Minor County cricket club (perhaps with himself as captain) in the East Riding.....may I ask who would provide the funds if such a club was created?* And the writer recalled that separation from political Lincolnshire in 1974 had been opposed by three-quarters of the people in polls held at the time.

Small wonder that one group whose efforts served to support historic York-shire was not a Yorkshire group at all. The mood which led to the founding of the North Lincolnshire Association in 1977 was aptly summed up by Michael Brotherton, MP for Louth, writing to the YRS the same year: *It would not be an exaggeration to say that at least 95% of the population of South Humberside regard themselves in fact as being resident in North Lincolnshire. We sympathise greatly with the plight of your members in the East Riding, and our concern is shown by our great desire to have nothing to do with them whatsoever!* 'Nothing', that is, under the umbrella of local government. For the writer's view, and that of the NLA, was that Humberside should be abolished. The Association was the new County's most implacable opponent. It feared the size and power of Hull; it saw a natural bias towards the more populous north bank in the distribution of resources; and it wanted nothing less than a new county of its own, with its own name: 'North Lincolnshire'.

To this end its members were prepared to cooperate with anyone — even Yorkshiremen — whose objectives helped to further their own. The establishment of a liaison committee was reported, involving NLA, EYAG and YRS: *Grand Alliance to fight for 'lost' Yorks;* and the local press described a colourful meeting at the Yorkshire/Lincolnshire border (Map 8) where a sign was planted showing 'real' county names and gifts were exchanged — Lincolnshire tulips and potatoes for a Hornsea mug, Wensleydale cheese, a Yorkshire Pudding mix (!) and a chocolate bar from York. But there was more to it than mere symbolism. Having already collaborated in the abortive campaign to change postal addresses, they agreed to canvass MPs, petition Whitehall and make submissions to the Boundary Commission Review.

For obvious reasons the NLA, more than the Yorkshire groups, tried to identify political discontent and focus it on change. And it must sometimes have felt remarkably close to success. It was its 1977 survey of public opinion, revealing a claimed 90% of the electorate in support, that prompted the Boundary Commission to advise the Secretary of State that a review of Humberside could be regarded as warranted — a procedure only invoked in 'wholly exceptional' situations. *Humberside Split Looks More Likely,* shouted the (London) Times (5 October 1982). It spoke of a *healthy disregard* for Yorkshiremen among generations of Lincolnshire people, of an *unholy alliance* between incompatibles (the view of the Secretary of the Association) and of *fierce resentment* at *money from the south going to hold up the decrepit north.*

By 1985, when a statutory review of Humberside had overtaken the proposal for a special one, the NLA claimed that a second, independent, poll (1983)[3] — part of a study of the feasibility of a south bank county sponsored by some of the local authorities — suggested 90% discontent. Underlying all the specific complaints was a general sense of alienation. Humberside was *the most obnoxious county in England;* south bank residents disliked *being forced together with Yorkshire people in an artificial county;* the addresses petition and the renaming of two Yorkshire Districts showed *it was hardly likely that any social engineering could succeed in Humberside:*

Even in the Anglo-Saxon period Lincolnshire was part of the Kingdom of Mercia, while north of the Humber (as the name implies) they were in Northum-

YORKSHIRE DAY
AUGUST 1ST

CELEBRATING THE <u>WHOLE</u> COUNTY OF YORK
- from Middlesbrough to Sheffield,
from Sedbergh to Hull -
IN ITS THREE HISTORIC RIDINGS

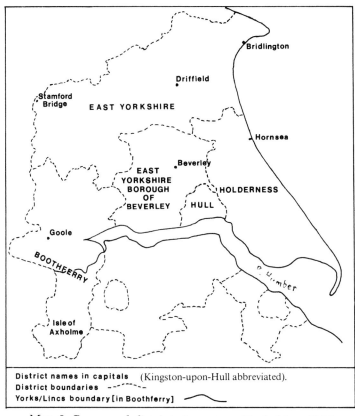

Map 8. Re-named districts in eastern Yorkshire, 1981.

EAST
RIDING
ALLIANCE

The eagle of integrity, the
sheaf of prosperity.

bria. (Note the dismissive 'they'). So romantic an appeal to distant roots —
among all the prosaic business of 'services' — must have staggered modern
metropolitan man at the DoE.

The Case for Democracy: East Riding Alliance

Like John Fisher before him, Michael Peck of Beverley had to contemplate the
changes in Yorkshire with the special feelings of one returning from abroad; but
since the year of his arrival was 1979, not 1971, he was denied any chance to
protest in advance: the East Riding had already, it seemed, been demolished
and Yorkshire disfigured. It was natural to look for reasons; and the fate of his
beloved hometown seemed to throw light on the wider situation. For it now had
no Council of its own. Instead its affairs were entrusted to a body representing a
population (101,348 — 1971 Census) six times that of the town itself. The name
of that body — 'Borough of Beverley District Council' — was no consolation
either. Indeed it was itself part of the deception — getting people to think that
local government was more local, and more historic, than it actually was. The
removal of power from the level where knowledge and understanding existed
only served to weaken democracy. And it had all happened in an undemocratic,
'top-down', way. Like the treatment of Yorkshire, it showed there was 'something wrong, politically and philosophically'. It could never have come about if
sufficient power had rested with the localities in the first place.

Such were the convictions which led to the founding of the East Riding
Alliance. Its objects were not only to undo the worst effects of 1974 but to
promote a system in which such aberrations could not occur. This would
involve the transfer of power to the parishes. Let control be vested in local units
providing directly whatever services they were competent to provide and join-
ing forces with others to secure those requiring larger populations. Essentially
things should operate outward and upward from the democratic base of the
historic local community.

The ERA's approach to the situation was set out in a letter of welcome to a
meeting with the Ridings Society and other pro-Yorkshire bodies held in
February 1981. A new alliance was suggested *against all unwanted changes
affecting the folk of the East Riding of the County of York. And – of course – the
greatest single unwanted change imposed upon us and our Lincolnshire neighbours
has been the creation of unhistoric Humberside.*

'The East Riding of the County of York'. The use of the ancient title added
force to the word 'unhistoric', itself a bland enough term on the face of it, but
for those with any sense of a place and its past, a damning indictment.

But the change had also been 'unwanted', a fact which suggested a political
approach to its undoing. After noting that Humberside County Council had
recently voted again *obdurately and unanimously, to continue to so call themselves,* the meeting was invited to consider *action promising hope of ending their
control of the administrative County of Humberside by way of the elections in
May.* A month later, the Beverley Guardian could describe the ERA as a
political movement not only campaigning for a change of name but *opposed to
County Councillors who support the idea of a united Humberside. Although not*

seeking representation in the County Council elections in May, the Alliance would be supporting candidates sympathetic to their cause. Clearly this was Yorkshire's counterpart to the NLA — its only counterpart, making smaller ripples over a shorter period of time, but nevertheless seeking partition by political means.

And it failed. Years later, Mr. Peck could only report that both of the main parties had 'declared against the Ridings'. At national level, only the Liberal and Social Democratic parties seemed committed to the sort of community politics he believed in — a somewhat disconcerting situation for one who was basically a Conservative by conviction! He would draw some comfort, meanwhile, from the Post Office's indulgence: 'East Yorkshire' seemed now a respected address, with even more respect to Beverley as simply 'Yorkshire'.

The Price of Democracy: Yorkshire Countrywomen's Association

The Spring 1988 issue of 'The Yorkshire Countrywoman' tells of a carol service at Whitby arranged by 'North Riding members' and attended by women 'from the three Ridings of Yorkshire'; and a former Chairman recalls how, five years back, the Association had begun with 'nothing except a determination to keep the County of Yorkshire alive'.

Supervising the mailing of the magazine are the two Honorary Secretaries. It is the sort of thing these two same ladies used to do for the Yorkshire Federation of Women's Institutes — for half the sixty years of its existence — this, and arranging musical evenings, a craft exhibition, a visit to the Edinburgh Festival and so on. They will soon be preparing for Yorkshire Day, a relatively new institution, like the Association itself. For the County that is now celebrated on 1st August each year is the Yorkshire of the YCA, organised in three Ridings, each with its own Committee devising activities for its own local Branches. For the YCA, places and names did not change with local government. Its 45 North Riding Branches include Redcar and Marske-by-the-sea; its East Riding ones (26) are all in places administered by Humberside County Council. Among its aims is 'to preserve the heritage of Yorkshire' — that same Yorkshire which the Women's Institute, belatedly in the 1980s, was forced to desert, leaving many who were loyal to it no option but to form their own association.

At the personal level it was a tragic business. As people tell of the success of the YCA — after only a brief life, more than 5000 members in over 120 Branches, plus a healthy bank balance — there is no gloating. *It is not a matter of winning; I was a member of the WI for 30 years.* The eventual rallying-point for the Association, Mrs Totty of Hawksworth, had opposed separation at first, even though the members had shown what they thought of the National Committee's instruction to divide into five new county federations (2687 in favour, 14209 for staying as they were). The decision to leave did not come until it was clear that Yorkshire was not the only thing at stake: it was a choice between democracy and authoritarianism, between 'London' and ordinary people. The last straw came with the National Federation's decision that Yorkshire members should not sit together at national conferences at the Albert Hall: *It was like punishing us for being naughty girls. With everything else that has happened it has shattered my faith in the national leadership.*

Everything else that has happened. The dark phrase was clarified in a letter from the then Chairman of the Association, Mrs Wynne Smith. The showdown with Yorkshire — 8 years after the 1974 reforms — had been ugly, even crude. 'London' had given notice that it would take legal action to dissolve the Yorkshire Federation, as it was empowered to do by its constitution and the Charity Commissioners' rules. Yorkshire was the biggest in the WI, with 22,000 members, its own HQ and 9 paid staff. The premises were to be sold, the staff sacked and the County split into six, corresponding with the new local government areas (North Yorkshire was to have two).

Many members felt that the implementation of the national policy on new boundaries was particularly unfair to Yorkshire — and unnecessary as well. But, as the Chairman put it, *they concluded that they had no power against their centralised organisation except that of their membership and subscription, and although many were devoted WI members their wish was to keep their identity as a Yorkshire organisation. They broke away from the WI in 1983 and formed the YCA.*

At that point each local Branch had had to decide its own future. Democracy versus oligarchy was an easy choice. So was that between Yorkshire and the new local government. But leaving the WI was a different matter. There were the many years of service and loyalty, the friends and colleagues. There was doubt about an uncertain future. Above all, there were the physical assets — premises, equipment, money — which under WI rules ceased to belong to a Branch once its affiliation ceased. So some — Flamborough, for instance, which owned its Hall — decided to stay....an honourable decision, like that of those who opted otherwise.

What lay behind the national policy to impose new counties? Officially the objective was *to ease administration and communication problems.* A YCA member suggested the motive was financial: they wanted local authority grants. (Yorkshire had never relied on them, and the YCA neither received nor wanted any ...*Members who are happy with what they get will pay for it).* The Ridings Society thought it discerned shadier motives — the Centre's fear of the largest Federation prompting a desire to 'divide and rule'. Whatever the true reasons, the National Federation's dealings with Yorkshire must be judged one of the crassest overreactions to the local government reforms on view. They are a prime example of politics being allowed to trespass on ground which does not belong to it, of democracy trampled upon, of faithfulness betrayed.

As for the founding members of the YCA, let the Yorkshire Post, recalling comment on a far more unequal contest long ago[4], have the last word: *It amounts to a unilateral declaration of Yorkshire independence. It may not be war – but it is magnificent. It is impossible to withhold admiration and respect from members who are prepared to abjure a lifetime's loyalty to the Women's Institute for what they see as the greater good.*

Footnote: those who remained in the WI did not allow their identity to be submerged. Geography required two Federations, not one, in the administrative area of Humberside. The one to the North of the river is called the East Yorkshire Federation.

FOOTNOTES

[1] The largest Yorkshire pudding on record — 20ft x 7ft, with 1200 eggs — was produced at Barnsley in 1986.

[2] They should: Chaucer, 600 years before, knew: *Lordynges, there is in Yorkshire, as I gesse, A mershee countree called Holdernesse.* (Summoner's Tale) (He wasn't really guessing, just stuck for a rhyme).

[3] An 'unscientific' poll, as R. J. Waller, author of the study conceded.

[4] 'C'est magnifique, mais ce n'est pas la guerre'. Marshal Bosquet, on the Charge of the Light Brigade, 1854.

CHAPTER 7: FIGHTING BACK

Not long after the YCA rebellion, '1974' became an open sore in several areas where county names were new. Identity — the effect of unfamiliar titles and broken ties — seemed an important factor, even if there were plenty of the usual grumbles about inefficiency. In one very ancient and historic Yorkshire place the causes of unrest were not altogether clear.

Heart's Content? Traffic lights control movement over the old bridge near the site of Harold's famous victory over the Danes in 1066. The large village of Stamford Bridge stands on the East bank of the Derwent, for centuries the boundary between East and North Ridings. Its history and location at Yorkshire's heart long made it a symbol of the County itself. Now, though but a few miles from the city of York (North Yorkshire), it is administered under Humberside.

In 1984 the villagers had the chance to vote on their situation — in a referendum held to decide whether to have the place transferred. Over 1000 had petitioned for a poll, about half the electorate. Some felt their more natural ties were with North Yorkshire, especially with York, others that change would bring less efficient services. The debate was of long-standing; it was time to settle it.

On the day of decision a huge 58% voted and the result was clear-cut: North Yorkshire 460; Humberside 732. Put like that, it might seem that the issue had been identity, and that 'Yorkshire' had lost. *Who won the Battle of Stamford Bridge? Shock, horror, it was Humberside!* ran the tragi-comic headline in the Yorkshire Ridings Magazine.

But the campaign had really been about more practical matters. The nearness of York — and of Malton, the Ryedale District Centre — favoured change. But in the end people feared the disruption of children's education, the weakening of support for the elderly and infirm. They preferred the known to the unknown, even at the cost of higher rates — a tribute, no doubt, to the County Council.......and to their own District within it, which 3 years before had taken on a familiar name. Those who cared about the subject of identity knew that it had already received attention. 'North Wolds' had been replaced by 'East Yorkshire'. Their postal address had always been 'Stamford Bridge, York'. And facing them at the approach to the village, whenever they returned home from York, was a trio of signs on which Humberside was outnumbered by Yorkshire two to one, the last one, announcing 'East Riding of Yorkshire', having been placed there, in the grounds of the Swordsman Inn, by members of the Ridings Society.

Their Riding was indeed the East. The poll had offered them something with 'North' in its title. East is East and North is North, and though they meet at the river, they are not the same thing.

Neither are politics and identity the same. The second battle of Stamford Bridge appears to show that when you have paid due regard to the latter, you can have a sensible debate about the former.

Frayed Edges. Strangely, the two themes were to clash more sharply round Yorkshire's edges than at its historic heart. The sparking point was a review of the new areas, conducted by the Boundary Commission in 1985 and 1986, as provided for in the 1972 Act. Now was the time for any who felt themselves deprived of Yorkshire by their exclusion from the 'Yorkshires' to do something about it.

Not that it was made easy for them. The criteria for change emphasised *effective and convenient local government* rather than patriotic feeling, and the people whose opinions were directly sought were precisely those with a seeming vested interest in continuity — the local authorities themselves. Comments were, however, invited from *anyone else interested* and many, as we shall see, were forthcoming, from ordinary citizens vigilant enough to find out about the Review and dedicated enough to press their case.

Two languages at Sedbergh. Since 1974 the former Sedbergh Rural District of the West Riding has been governed by a body called the South Lakeland District Council, a title which explains some of the alienation felt by the area's inhabitants. For Sedbergh has no lake. The majestic Howgills, towering over the town to the north, are not Lakeland fells. Nearer than the likes of Coniston Old Man and High Street are the Yorkshire mountains, Whernside and Ingleborough. The place still lies within the Yorkshire Dales National Park (Map 9).

To the outsider, the strangest feature of the 1985/6 boundary debate there was the distance between people and councillors, a gap all the more remarkable because the community is so small — the Parish Councils of Sedbergh, Dent and Garsdale represented, respectively, 2233, 663 and 226 people. Yet however misleading signed petitions may be as a guide to public opinion, the gulf was unmistakable. In Sedbergh alone, the Sedbergh and District Action Group for Yorkshire claimed 1124 signatures from an electorate of 1917: the Parish Council's resolution in favour of Cumbria was taken by 10 votes to nil.

The fact is that those concerned with 'services' and those yearning for identity employ different tongues. Politicians see no need to speak the language of what they call 'sentiment'. The debate must be conducted in their kind of words, as the announcement of the Review had made clear.

The chance for the two sides to converse — other than in the letter columns of the Westmorland Gazette — came eventually in a public meeting. The decision to hold one itself demonstrated the 'distance', for it was taken by precisely 5 votes to 4. Perhaps the Councillors doubted whether anyone would turn up. Not a single person had attended 14 years before, claimed one, even though *we did all we could to make people know what we were doing* (ie taking Sedbergh into

94

Cumbria). Council and people so far apart. Would they have come, in 1971, if they had known their identity was at stake? — if they had known the implications of *what we were doing?* (Note the undemocratic, distancing tone of that phrase).

Probably. For to a meeting thus grudgingly staged no fewer than 150 people now came, with others unable to get in. They were to hear and speak the language of 'services': Sedbergh's loss of its Council Offices and its Registrar; high rates; tourism — playing second fiddle to the Lake District; and always Kendal (Cumbria) nearby, offering shops, work, leisure, and brooding over all. No vote was taken, and the Group's request for a poll was refused. Evidently the Council was too sure of itself — or mistrustful of a wayward public.

Back to Yorkshire Debate not Conclusive was the Gazette's verdict — a view evidently not shared by the Council which proceeded now to its whitewash vote, duly informing the District Council which had already declared itself more interested in the views of elected representatives than in 1100 signatures.

Back to Yorkshire. Like the Action Group's own title, those words take us well beyond politics. *Sedbergh for the Craven District of the Administrative County of North Yorkshire* — a more accurate statement of the consequences of success — would have missed the point. The Guardian's headline did not miss it: *Yorkshire Parishes Petition to go home.* Nor did the Yorkshire Post: *Move Border plea by county exiles.* The group's prime movers, David Isger, originally from Halifax, and Nancy Walsh spoke of 'not belonging', of Lake District people as 'alien'. It was the other language, the one the politicians did not comprehend. (One of these, not around in 1974 but now Sedbergh's man on the District Council, was sure that the unrest could be traced to the recent imposition of a charge in the town's car park!).

Perhaps the DoE, after all, would listen. The Action Group had no option but to try. Their written submission used both languages. Through the document's political surface time and again the theme of identity breaks like rock through the Pennine turf: *our birthright has been taken away.....we have been taken into a different culture.....historically, geographically and sentimentally* (the word used unashamedly) *we are Yorkshire people and that is where we belong .....if the boundaries could be put back..we would then be at home.*

Then the peroration: *we appeal to you to put right this injustice of our birthright and deep feeling of separation from our own Yorkshire Dales people, with whom we belong. North Yorkshire, Craven District, are our own and understand us and our needs, indeed we are one with each other. How on earth can a Yorkshire Dales market town belong to Cumbria and the Lake District?*

As to all the instances of misgovernment she quoted, would Mrs Walsh have mentioned them if they had occurred under a 'Yorkshire' council? Perhaps they would not have happened. In any case you can put up with a lot more if only you feel 'at home'. What she said to the Guardian summed it up for so many. *This is not political. I am just a Yorkshire woman who was bunged into Cumbria against her will.*

Emotion at Yarm. Cleveland County covers much Yorkshire land (Map 10) — much more than Cumbria — but it displays few public traces of the fact.

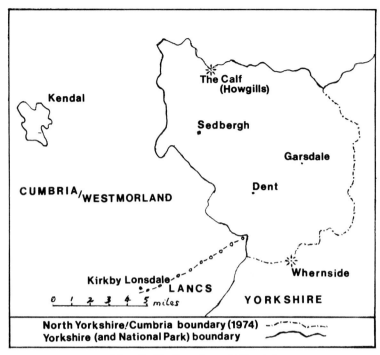

Map 9. *Sedbergh and Kendal.*

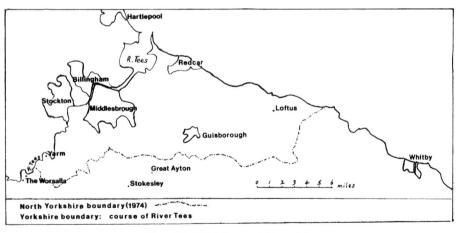

Map 10. *Whitby and Teesside.*

Yorkshire plays cricket there, but no-one has tried to change any of the Districts' names — not even 'Langbaurgh' (Indeed, what Yorkshire name could they have used, for an area lying to the north of the northern boundary of something called 'North Yorkshire'?) Here the TV Channel is 'Tyne-Tees', and the official Region is the 'North', with Newcastle, not Leeds, as its Centre. The Yorkshire Dales National Park may include Sedbergh, but no such comforting shadow falls across Redcar and Guisborough.

Could pro-Yorkshire feeling have survived after 12 years of alien influence? In April 1986 the Northern Echo (Darlington) gave the answer: *Of the many opinions Yorkshiremen dislike hearing about themselves, being told they're not Yorkshiremen probably takes priority.* It was reporting the annual Parish Meeting at Yarm, North Riding, currently in the Stockton District of Cleveland. The previous year this had attracted 1 member of the public. Now there were over 200, most of them insistent that the people have a chance to vote on leaving Cleveland — so as to guide the Parish Council in its reply to the Boundary Commission. The Council, for its part, desired neither vote nor guidance. It knew what to say to the Commission: 'No change'. But over 1400 had signed a 'Return to Yorkshire' petition, and they were not to be fobbed off. *They have just decided to spend £1600 on a poll,* said the scornful Chairman. *Then, it was their money,* commented the Echo.

Small wonder the Chairman was perplexed. True, Yarm's rates were high, but the County Treasurer confirmed that more was spent on it than it paid. The broad High St still reminds you of Yorkshire places like Northallerton and Skipton, but turn a corner and you see the mushrooming estates whose residents commute to workaday Teesside. Since 1974, while Sedbergh has stood still, Yarm's 4000 have become 8000, $3/4$ of them new to the place since North Riding County Council days. Why were they not content to stay in the County which now gave them their livelihood?

In the meeting itself, the language of employment and shopping grappled with that of identity and pride. Reason versus emotion? Not entirely. The unsentimental men from County Hall let their slips show now and again — to the amusement of the Echo's man. The Treasurer, he wrote, after claiming to give the unemotive view, said that the nearest North Yorkshire Fire Station was twice the distance of the Cleveland one and asked the assembled townsfolk whether they wanted their houses to burn for twice as long. *(One hoped,* said the Reporter, *he wasn't going to get emotive).* Thankfully, he conceded that Cleveland would not let Yarm burn to the ground.

Later on it was the politicians' tempers that burned. *If the people of Yarm want appalling services, which is what North Yorkshire provides, that is up to them,* said Cleveland's leader. 'Scurrilous', retorted his opposite number, the aptly-named Councillor Clout, who remarked that no one was trying to get out of North Yorkshire while round its edges people were trying to get in.

For Nigel Wilkin, a boy of 13 in 1974, emotion was nothing to be ashamed of anyway. *Sir – I have grown up in Yarm, and in 1974 was disgusted when the town was rudely and undemocratically taken out of its home county.....no one was seriously consulted. It just happened. People gradually lost their identity as yorkshire people, and the pride they had in the history and heritage of Yarm as*

97

Yarm High Street.

The battle for Yarm.

*an ancient North Riding town disappeared..... Yarm on the historical map of England
is a Yorkshire town. No government or parliament should have the right to change
that. Are our children and our children's children to lose forever the pride they had in
this Yorkshire town?*

It was his letter to the press inviting people to sign the petition. At the meeting
he received a standing ovation. He asked the Parish Council — *respectfully, like
all Yorkshiremen,* as the Echo put it — to resign if they didn't follow the wishes
of the people.

As for the Poll, in a mere 5 hours 41.7% voted — well above local election
levels. 1675 said 'yes' and 682 'No'. And the strange thing was that the question
they were answering — words approved by a hostile Council — was such as to
favour Mr. Wilkin's cause. It was his language. Not, *Do you wish Yarm's
services to be provided by North Yorkshire County Council?* but, *Do you wish to
return to Yorkshire?* Colin Holt, who had assured the Parish Meeting that they
were still in the only North Riding (and Yorkshire) that mattered, one that was
immune to Acts of Parliament, would have queried that word 'return'. Still, he
rejoiced, no doubt, in the victory of those who valued their roots.

But had anything been achieved? Six weeks on, Nigel Wilkin was pleading
with his 'own' folk through that mouthpiece of his homeland, the Yorkshire
Post: *Today, as I compile a report for the Boundary Commission, the parishioners
of Yarm have the support of no political party, parish or borough councillor or even
their local MP who lives in the town.... Yarm has voted democratically to return to
its Yorkshire roots. Will someone support us?*

Pragmatism at Loftus. On the face of it, the small town of Loftus is not only in
Cleveland but proud of it, for 'Loftus-in-Cleveland' is the name quoted in the
Council's letterhead. But the word has different senses, and this one is the
ancient ''cliff-land' of the North Riding, not the new county which stole its
name. Loftus is certainly in the 'cliff-land'......for ever. A mile or two to the East,
sea-gulls wheel and cry in the mist where Boulby Cliff, the highest in Yorkshire
— indeed, the second highest in all England — falls 660 feet into an icy North
Sea.

The debate here was unsentimental. No wonder: it is an unsentimental sort of
place. Beneath that North Sea men toil in potash mines at temperatures over
90°, while management in the cliff-top offices grumble about the County's high
rates. There are steel-works nearby, and a tradition of quarrying and brick-
making. Alum has been mined, and ironstone. Historic links with the new
county's capital are obvious and fundamental. For it was on the mineral
resources of this area that the infant Middlesbrough, a mere fledgling in 1800,
began to feed and grow to a size that called for local administration separate
from the rest of the North Riding. Like Middlesbrough — and indeed like
Cleveland — Loftus is predominantly Labour. And if that seems a strange
point to make, it is mentioned because here, while both sides spoke the
language of 'services' — of politics, in that sense — one of them employed an
accent not found elsewhere, that of the political party.

The first issue, again, was participative democracy. For when the Council
resolved to tell the Boundary Commission that *the people of Loftus....had no*

wish to become part of North Yorkshire people objected to finding out about it only through reading the local weekly, the Whitby Gazette. They wanted a voice in the matter. Once again there was a petition, a long and stormy debate in a crowded Town Hall and a request for a Poll, at first refused, then finally agreed.

As before, those favouring change were accused of being driven by emotion, but in truth they showed very little. One letter to the press asserted that *though most of us would love to live in Yorkshire....the reason...most want out of Cleveland is purely the ridiculously high rates.* Another, having talked of 'roots', dwelt on the extravagance of the Council's free bus-passes. A luminously orange poster might speak of voting Loftus 'back into Yorkshire' but the campaign leaflet, delivered to each household, resumed the theme of high rates for poor services. The Campaign's very title struck the same unsentimental note: not 'Loftus for Yorkshire' but......'Get out of Cleveland'.

The other side appealed to emotions of another kind: compassion and fear. A leaflet from the town's County Councillor, who was also the Vicar, reminded those objecting to high rates that *civilised living looks beyond self to the needs of all.* In its own leaflet the Loftus Labour Party shouldered patriotism aside: those wanting change were voting not for North Yorkshire but for Mrs Thatcher. *Who do you want to run your services, Tory or Labour?*

So Loftus too had its Poll. Its question, unlike Yarm's, was low-key : *Should the Boundary Commission be informed that Loftus Parish be withdrawn from Cleveland County and form part of North Yorkshire?* But the 'Out' party won, if by only 24 votes (1153 — 1129), and on a low poll (32.64%); and that night they were in euphoric mood, for at least they had made a point about democracy and taught their representatives a lesson.

Or so they might have thought until they looked, once again, in their newspaper: *Yorks vote snub* ran the headline. The Boundary Commission was to be asked by the Council to take no action *as 84% of the electorate did not vote to go into North Yorkshire.* It was an unusual way of presenting the figures — adding the non-voters to those against!

Landslide at Guisborough. The verdict of the last Cleveland plebiscite was clear enough. Guisborough voted 4950 to 953 to leave. Here, at least, Council and people were agreed. The former, as the local paper put it, *supported the move out, despite being the ancient capital of Cleveland....*a phrase which both confused, grammatically, the Council with the town, and mistook one kind of Cleveland for another. For there was nothing paradoxical about the Council's approach. The old headquarters of the hill country had, since 1974, stood on the very edge of a county which had tried to usurp the identity of that country. Guisborough would not be deserting its own Cleveland by leaving that. If anything, its 'ancient capital' status was a motive for quitting, not for staying put.

Not surprisingly, here sentiment counted. Did not the local accent resemble country speech to the south? The place's Yorkshire tradition was 900 years old. It 'belonged' there.

Such views seemed strange at first when spoken in a Scots accent, that of a leader of the Campaign, one who had not known Guisborough in North Riding days. But tradition often matters a lot to those who move in, sometimes more than to those who never left. *Nobody knows where Cleveland is,* said Councillor Alexander.

The other language, meanwhile, counted for little. On polling day people were 'streaming' out of the Council estates to vote. *Don't give us facts about services* (the County Council had issued a special edition of 'the Clevelander' for the occasion).....*we just want to get back into Yorkshire,* seemed to be their attitude. The numbers voting — at holiday-time, and with a mere five hours available — were unprecedented. Some came late, to locked doors; the coffee flasks of harassed officials stood unopened. It was not like a local government election......

Good Copy. Whatever the real influence of pro-Yorkshire feeling on these North Riding events, it suited the media to angle things that way. Even the London Times could bother to report remote provincial controversies if the language of roots and heritage could be employed (and especially when the dish could be garnished with mustard — a slanging match between two county council leaders). It spoke of the strong desire of 'exiles' to return and to win back their birthright.

Metropolitan readers' ready sympathy with such feelings could evidently be assumed, even if their assumptions about Yorkshiremen might tempt them to accept the reported claim of Cleveland's leader that the votes against his county had quite a lot to do with their rate bills.

A Gesture from Pendle. If new county concepts like 'Cumbria' and 'Cleveland' felt alien, small wonder that 'Lancashire', of all things, should. Eventually news came that pro-Yorkshire signatures had been collected in Earby and Barnolds-wick — 1250, in 18 shops, in a mere fortnight. The organiser, Councillor C. Nolan, intended to convey the fact to the Boundary Commission. Not that he had any hope of success: local politicians, apart from himself, were indifferent to the issue. Not so, the people. He estimated that three-quarters were on his side. And so sure was he that 'sentiment' lay behind this that he was keen to show there were other factors too. (Doubtless he had heard that for the Commission, as for Edith Cavell, patriotism was not enough). His area was getting a raw deal from the new Pendle District: not rich itself, it was being used to prop up even poorer places like Nelson and Colne. (Map 4). The signatures would at least enable him to say he had tried to do something.

A Press announcement soon seemed to confirm that that was all he would be able to claim. Under *Yorks draws the line on Boundary,* the local paper reported North Yorkshire County Council's message to the Commission that it wanted no change in West Craven.

Heads and Hearts. It was indeed hard to foresee any changes in accord with the people's verdicts arising from the polls held in 1985/6. The Commission, it is true, said it would consider: *whether or not ...a boundary accords with the wishes of the local inhabitants* and such things as *a sense of separation from other areas,* *stemming from social, geographical, economic and cultural influences*[1]. Clearly it was interested in feelings, in psychology, a field to which the 1974 reforms and their sequel had paid scant attention hereabouts. But whose opinion was it to heed? The politicians, in every place except Guisborough, were against change.

Besides, the Secretary of State had warned against putting the clock back. The guidance he had given to the Commission held no comfort for those wishing to 'return home'. Tradition, in his view, had already played too great a part (if not, perhaps, in Yorkshire?). *The boundaries adopted in 1972...were for the most part set by reference to pre-existing ....boundaries, some of them of considerable antiquity. Changes in the pattern of development.....may well require the revision of some of these boundaries, and the Secretary of State takes the view that the primary purpose of the present review should be to consider the need for such alterations*[2].

A Year of Hope

1986 was nevertheless a time of encouragement for lovers of Yorkshire. News of the patriotic polls coincided with Government action which looked as though it might be helpful. For it undid some of the work of 1974 by abolishing the County Councils of West and South Yorkshire. Some people, it is true, were disposed to lament their passing, and on patriotic grounds. *Look what they're doing to our Rose!,* cried the Bradford Evening Telegraph, on Good Friday, 1985, in a special edition of the long-defunct Yorkshire Observer. First 1974, now this! But others saw things quite differently. The disappearance of 'South Yorkshire' and 'West Yorkshire' would surely confirm what they had long proclaimed: that administrative geography was unreal. Evidently such fragile places could appear and vanish in the space of 12 short years....while historic Yorkshire, which had briefly lent them its name, persisted unaffected. Perhaps, when the mist had cleared, the landscape of the West Riding might even be revealed.

So much for speculation. The reality proved quite different. Traditionalists had obviously been misled by the media's shorthand references to abolishing 'the counties', when only the county councils, and many of their employees, were to be affected. Abolition day, 1 April 1986, came and went without a change in any map or textbook. Major services like transport, police and fire brigades continued under West and South Yorkshire labels, and covering the same areas — which also retained those other county emblems, their Lords Lieutenant and High Sheriffs. The nature of a political county was thus clarified. A council was not, after all, indispensable to it; and survival without one seemed to strengthen, not weaken, its geographical status.

Addresses again. Nevertheless the 1986 reforms saw the question of addresses surprisingly reopened. Since places remained unchanged this clearly was not called for; and it must be assumed that memories of the Humberside furore eight years before had thrown the Post Office off balance. Certainly the consultation now undertaken suggested a high degree of sensitivity; for in addition to the circular to MPs, local authorities and business users, a market research survey of the general public was conducted.

The result was a public announcement, in January 1986, to the affect that no consensus for change had been found in West or South Yorkshire and that existing postal addresses would therefore remain. Out of a representative sample of 1000 in West Yorkshire 10% actively wanted a change — to 'Yorkshire' or 'West Riding' — one-fifth of them even if extra costs were involved. (Corresponding figures for South Yorkshire were 16% and one-third). 10% were said to see no point in change. The rest, presumably, were indifferent. Such figures, if they show anything, suggest that 'Yorkshire' is so much the most important word that any address which includes it is more or less acceptable; and 'West Yorkshire' is evidently close enough to 'West Riding' to produce rather more satisfaction than 'South Yorkshire'.

West Riding of Yorkshire. Meanwhile there appeared a Yorkshire champion from an unexpected quarter — the City Council of Leeds — 'unexpected' if only because it is naturally hard for those engaged in local government to conceive of a 'county' that does not run services (though the County of York itself offers a prime example).

Leeds now showed it had no such difficulty. It was not interested in using any new-fangled phrase. It not only 'preferred' 'West Riding of Yorkshire', it was going to have it, even though Leeds was important enough not to need a county at all in its letterhead. The City Council, like all recipients of mail, had a right to tell other people where they were to be found. If they did not know, who did?

The view is, wrote their Chief Officer to a protesting Post Office, *that 'West Riding of Yorkshire' should follow 'Leeds', not simply to preserve the tradition of 'Riding' but additionally in a vigorous attempt to retain the name 'Yorkshire' itself.......we may well find ourselves in an extraordinary position, with the East Riding apparently gone and South and West Yorkshire Councils about to disappear shortly – that the correct address of the largest centres of population and commerce will fail to identify this area as Yorkshire. The name will simply disappear except as it relates to rural North Yorkshire and smaller centres in the West and South. We have noted the points in your letter and understand them: but the simple truth is that without some positive stand now, then Yorkshire may become as historic in the minds of the inhabitants of Watford and its suburbs as 'Rutland'.*

A further request to reconsider was brushed aside by an inexorable Council. A Labour member described the request as a slap in the face. A Tory said he was proud to have been born in Leeds, in the West Riding of Yorkshire, and he wanted the West Riding back. A Deputy Mayor had the precious words used at his swearing in. It was one issue that united all parties. The local Member of the European Parliament joined in: *Yorkshire-born people all over the world use the words 'West Riding' even though Edward Heath tried to destroy its use and re-write Yorkshire history.* The Halifax Courier rejoiced, referring to the Post Office as a 'spoilsport', to the Ridings as 'those lovely old thirds of the County', and to the need to ensure that they 'go on for ever'.

Eleven years on, and the Whitehall hatchet men are poised to strike again

Look how they're pruning our rose

April 1, 1974 now seems a highly appropriate date for Local Government Reorganisation. We say All Fool's day 11 years ago meant local government DIS-organisation for Yorkshire. And next year it's going to get worse...

WE Yorkshire folk have the reputation of being obstreperous and standing no nonsense, especially from the purveyors of red tape.

Well, that's the myth we like to foster. In fact, when it comes to keeping intact the identity of our beloved Yorkshire, we have let the Whitehall wallies walk all over us.

They have done their level best to destroy Yorkshire as a county, and we have let them do it. Eleven years ago they split it into numerous bits and tried to bamboozle folk that they were not really Yorkshiremen after all.

When they invented the territories now known as Cleveland and Humberside, did they ask the inhabitants if it was all right with them? They did not.

When they nudged little places like Barnoldswick and Dentdale across the border, did they inquire whether the folk there wanted to be Lancastrians? They did not.

Unhappy

They even tacked on to Humberside, part of North Lincolnshire. Perhaps that was Whitehall's way of committing themselves to the Humber Bridge, but it brought together an unhappy alliance of communities.

Even the finest bridge in the world has not brought them together in spirit. Despite all the protests, nothing has been done.

Yet why not? What does it matter to Whitehall if Humberside is called East Yorkshire? Who'd care in London if Cleveland felt like styling itself (with apologies to a well-known

Map labels: Lost to Durham · Lost to Cleveland · Middlesbrough · Lost to Cumbria · Sedbergh · Richmond · Scarborough · North Riding · East Riding · Harrogate · Skipton · York · Bridlington · Lost to Lancashire · Hull · Barnsley · Lost to Humberside · Sheffield · Lost to Greater Manchester

BEFORE AND AFTER. Bits of Yorkshire have been scattered far and wide by reorganisation. West Yorkshire is just a shadow of its former self. South Yorkshire is

*1986: How the "Yorkshire Observer" saw it.
By courtesy of the Bradford Telegraph & Argus*

Yorkshire Evening Post

Restore the Ridings!

Compromise. The city councillors had seen no need to say what they meant by 'West Riding'. By implication the name applied to the same area as ever it did, to Sedbergh, Barnoldswick and all. It was the Ridings Society's message, now given proud endorsement. The man who wanted the West Riding back could feel he had never lost it; his place was still there.

A different note, though springing from the same motives, was now sounded by the Yorkshire Evening Post. Its Editor saw in the abolition of the county councils a chance to RESTORE THE RIDINGS; and he would be precise about areas. Himself the author, in happier times, of a book on the North Riding — not a work, needless to say, about how that delectable land was governed — he would nevertheless do a deal with the new politics. Let West and South Yorkshire be jointly known as 'West Riding', North Yorkshire become 'North Riding' and North Humberside 'East Riding'. Let readers use their new 'Riding' address, urge MPs to refer to the Ridings, press parliamentary candidates about the issue and insist that other Yorkshire cities follow the example of Leeds. On the day the campaign was launched (and every day since) the paper's official imprint included 'West Riding of Yorkshire' in its address.

The Editor regretted the necessary pragmatism of his proposals: the omission of Sedbergh, West Craven, Saddleworth and Cleveland — 'the amputations of 1974' — from the new Ridings. But get the Ridings back and it would be easier to *regain these terrories one day.* No local government reforms were required. *All we have to do is to start using OUR Ridings as part of OUR addresses again.*

For all its pragmatism the Campaign left practical questions unanswered. In the west and north official recognition might well, some day, follow popular use of, and demand for, old names; but would Humberside County Council ever be persuaded to acknowledge 'East Riding' for what was only part of its territory? Eight years earlier 120,000 signatures had failed to achieve anything tangible. If, on the other hand, official recognition did not matter in the east, why pay regard to political areas anywhere? Could not the YEP print real maps, for instance? Must cartography always reflect local government?

The Campaign's assumption that it must, made for other difficulties in Humberside. For Boothferry District had to be dealt with as a whole. Yet only the northern part of it is (so to speak) in Yorkshire; the remainder — the ancient Isle of Axholme — is (likewise) in Lincolnshire. *Come and join us - Yorkshire urges limbo island* ran the YEP's headline. The islanders, spurning such an honour, pressed on with a campaign of their own — to leave Humberside indeed, but for Lincs. (See Map 8 in Chap 6).

Elsewhere the proposals were well publicised and mostly well received. Under the heading *Yorkshiremen Renew Campaign for Ridings* the Ridings Society's Secretary informed the mainly southern readership of the Daily Telegraph that it was a fallacy to tell people they were not somewhere when they knew they were: *Our heritage is as important to Yorkshire men and women as the Monarchy is.* A phone-in to Radio Leeds showed a 10 to 1 majority for the YEP's Editor. The brewers, Tetleys, famed for the car slogan *Yorkshire born and brewed,* were said to be ordering their 1100 pubs to start using the Ridings in addresses. From one lady's letter to the paper you get a feeling of that larger pre-war England whose geography was among the enduring certainties people lived by: *Although I am not Yorkshire born, I have lived here for 40 years and am intensely interested in the revival of the West Riding in our address. From just after the Great War until 1928 I heard such a lot about the Ridings in history and geography lessons because I had teachers who often visited Yorkshire. When I heard that by a stroke of the pen they would be eradicated I did not want to believe what I was reading.*

Others rejected the very idea that a pen could do any such thing. *It is time,* wrote one, *that Yorkshire folk started fighting back on this issue taking every opportunity to proclaim that the County of Yorkshire extends from the Humber to the Tees.* Another, from Loftus, spurned the Campaign. It was 'absolutely scandalous' to try to restore the use of titles without including those 'unceremoniously kicked out' in 1974; the old Ridings still existed.......*if many of us are not to feel abandoned into outer darkness let's forget the 'new' Ridings idea and go for the restoration of Yorkshire as it was before 1974.* And he signed himself, poignantly, 'I. Landless'. The ROOTS organisation would have preferred a campaign which said the Ridings were alive, and only needed Yorkshire loyalty to make others realise it.

Another group supported the YEP's approach but only as a step on the way to the real goal. *The way forward is to adapt our unique Ridings, embrace our county friends on the Tees and bring alive that pride again,* wrote a Malton man somewhat vaguely. *More power to your elbow in the campaign to re-establish our ancient boundaries,* was the toast of an 'exile' in Essex. A Leeds man seemed to hit the nail on the head. *I would also like to see places like Middlesbrough, Saltburn and Dent back into local government areas based on Yorkshire.*

Local government based on Yorkshire. Crucial words. The YEP was prepared to do things the other way round with the best of intentions. If history and tradition do not 'fit' local politics, must the two be made to match? And if so, which of the two must 'move'?

A Sheffield (and Rotherham) afterthought. A fine souvenir edition of the YEP, 'Restore the Ridings' (June 1986), proudly showed photographs of all Yorkshire's major inland towns (and many minor places too). All, that is, except one (two). Unlike Hutton-le-Hole and Thornton Dale, Sheffield (and Rotherham) was not there. And in the text the only references to one of England's great cities occurred in parenthesis. Leeds, said the Leeds-based paper, was the *de facto* capital of its 'new' West Riding *whatever Sheffield folk might say.*

Hardly the way to foster the allegiance of an important place whose Yorkshireness might well be frail enough already. For Sheffield is not part of the favoured literary/media image of dales and moors, mills and mines. It is a long way from what a Sheffield man[3] called the 'heart and homeland', Ilkley and Otley. Its influence extends south to the Midlands, its Health Authority is the Trent, its playground, the Peak. Once it was Yorkshire CCC's first-ever host. Now its most famous ground, Bramall Lane, scene of battles as dourly 'Yorkshire' as the canopy above (not skies — you couldn't see them), has banished the game for good.

We have seen what happens to large places on the edge, even when estuaries bar the way. Yet Sheffield, a greater place than Middlesbrough or even Hull, with scarcely a brook, a rivulet to stop it, remained a wholly Yorkshire authority. 'South Yorkshire', whatever traditionalists might feel, gave it a separate sphere from Leeds. So two cheers for 1974. Well one then.

FOOTNOTES

[1] DoE Circular 33/78, Para 14 and Annex B. (quoted in 12/84).

[2] DoE Circular 12/84, Para 12.

[3] Roy Hattersley. Op.Cit.

CHAPTER 8: TAKING STOCK

Life after Politics. At its highest point the Trans-Pennine motorway M62 passes for several miles through a wilderness of desolate rain-drenched moorland. It is an awesome place, inspiring thoughts of man's mortality and the transitoriness of things. It is also a worthy frontier — the word insists on itself, replacing 'boundary': forgetting the stream of lorries, you could think yourself somewhere like North-West India. There, at 1300 feet, stand two pillars, often mist-shrouded, one on each side of the road. They are of concrete, made to last; and embedded in each is a plaque and a large metal rose, the eastbound one white, the other red. *This plaque,* states the common inscription, *marks the boundary between the counties of York and Lancaster,* adding that the Queen unveiled it in October 1971 when the new road — 'the Lancashire-Yorkshire motorway' — was officially opened. A few yards further on down the Lancashire slope stands a rickety-looking notice, 'Greater Manchester County', a token of 1974. Did this flimsy device really supplant that red rose set in concrete? Should the pillar have been dismantled? What, in any case, have they to do with each other?

Ordinary people themselves gave the answer. Thousands went on watching Lancashire play cricket in 'Greater Manchester's' capital and saw nothing strange in that: and four-fifths of those questioned in a random Oldham poll gave Lancashire as the name of the place they felt themselves part of, aided and abetted by a consenting Post Office.

Yorkshire on the Ground

As for the White Rose, some say that what it stands for was abolished only three years after the pillars were erected, when 'the County of York's'[1] boundaries ceased to be endorsed by those of local government. Let us see what society had made of that half a generation later. We shall find that in place names, in social, commercial and cultural life, and especially in the mind, the White Rose lived. In sport sometimes controversially, and in literature often with misgiving, people would not let it die. More specifically, as the Red Rose was to be found in 'Greater Manchester', so Yorkshire was not to be excluded from 'Humberside'.

Or even from 'Durham', 'Cumbria' and 'Cleveland'. *This part of the North Riding has paid its rates to County Durham since 1974 but to the Tyke it is and always will be Yorkshire.* The writer was the landlord of The Rose and Crown at Mickleton in the almost forgotten Upper Tees valley (Map 11), where on 1 August the White Rose flag is flown, free Yorkshire puddings and parkin are on offer, and appropriate songs sung. *The village of Dent lies in one of Yorkshire's*

108

M62: Counties in concrete, 1971.

Dent – at the heart of "one of Yorkshire's loveliest valleys". Photo by courtesy of Cliff Megson.

loveliest valleys, ran the caption on a 1980s postcard. Was it a mistake, or an attempt to distinguish place from politics? The same doubt arose from a Guardian report headed *Unique cooperative cinema in North Yorkshire* and calling Redcar *a small seaside resort on the North Yorkshire coast.* Maybe the writer didn't know about Cleveland or thought his readers mightn't. Maybe he thought (with reason) that Cleveland, whatever it was, was in Yorkshire.

Deliberate mistakes. In the East any 'mistakes' could safely be assumed to be deliberate. OS Landranger Maps 101 and 106 now showed two 'East Yorkshire' Districts between them covering two-thirds of 'North Humberside'. As well as a Humberside Police Sinfonia there was an East Riding County Sinfonia (supported by Lincolnshire and Humberside Arts). You could also listen to Viking Radio, the commercial station, broadcasting to 'East Yorkshire and Lincolnshire' while its competitor addressed itself to 'Humberside'. (It would: Radio Humberside is its name). People joined an East Riding Flower Club, the East Yorkshire Family History Society, the Hull and East Riding Touring Club and so on. They could buy 'East Riding Farm Produce' and store it in the products of the East Riding Sack and Paper Co. They could not read 'Humberside Life' any more or attend a separate 'Humberside Show': both had folded some years back. While young people enjoyed a high social life in 'Humberside Young Farmers' (funded by the County) their fathers still belonged to the East Riding Branch of the NFU.

In brief, while the East Riding of the County of York was still, in the nineteen-eighties, (mostly) organised at political county level under 'Humberside', it retained a socio-geographic status of its own. Its people rode on East Yorkshire buses, used power from YEB, drank water from Yorkshire Water, watched YTV, supported Hull and East Riding Rugby Club, and attended hospitals run by the East Yorkshire Health Authority. Their children went to schools run by the East Riding Division. They walked the Yorkshire Wolds, spoke with Yorkshire accents (their own variety — there are many) and believed themselves Yorkshire people. This, at any rate, is the conclusion to be inferred from a small random 1984 poll taken in the streets of Goole (Humberside — but West Riding) where the only two people out of 40 prepared to disclaim such a belief turned out to be from Scotland and the Midlands.

Puzzling the Tourist. So much for the residents. Visitors actual and potential also found old names jostling new. One approach to the general problem is, of course, to say that Humberside (North) is in Yorkshire. The Shell Guide (1981), however, had it the other way about: *The East Riding of Yorkshire (now part of Humberside) is perhaps insufficiently appreciated by tourists.* (The Filey area of the East Riding, incidentally, is not in Humberside for anything). The title of the Tourist Board itself — 'Yorkshire and Humberside' — suggests that there is no overlap between old and new at all, but it is simply reflecting the sources of its funding and should therefore read, not 'Yorkshire', but 'the Yorkshires'. When it tried to impose the second half of its name on the countryside it often ran into trouble. The Borough of East Yorkshire would not follow the Board's description of Bridlington as a 'Humberside resort'. Indeed the Borough would not have had its new name had it been prepared to swallow things like that. You had to write to The Spa, Bridlington, East Yorkshire, for a brochure which promised a *warm Yorkshire welcome,* to a place making *the most of Yorkshire's holiday coast,* and offered cruises round Flamborough Head on the 'Yorkshire Belle' — nostalgic successor to the pre-war 'Yorkshireman'. A boarding house proprietor with the address 'Millington, East Riding of Yorkshire' insisted on the exclusion of his place from the 'Destination Humberside' Accommodation Guide. No one was seeking that 'grey area'. His customers, for their part, were coming to Yorkshire. Similar reasons prompted an 'East Riding Ranger' rail ticket, a Yorkshire Coast Farm holidays cooperative and an Enterprise Travel leaflet entitled 'Hull and East Yorkshire'. Punters were encouraged to *Go Racing in Yorkshire* at Ripon and.....Beverley, *Heritage Centre of the East Riding.* The Board's schizoid approach, meanwhile, emerged in a document describing Hornsea Mere as 'Yorkshire's largest lake' while an accompanying photograph called it the largest in 'Yorkshire and Humberside'. Was this one place or two? (Or four — the Yorkshires and Humberside?) If two, which was the Mere in? One sensible answer could be 'both', since Humberside (North) was itself in Yorkshire — with an administrative role. But if that was its role, why mention it in the context of holidays?

Yorkshire on the Field

Before reorganisation, at the end of 1971, the Craven Herald's weekly article by 'In Baulk' asked *Will there have to be a Boundary Commission for Snooker?* A timely question, on a thorny topic. For there is no more powerful source of identity than sport. Would the discontinuities of 1974 affect it? The new counties (and in terms of the legislation they were all new) were *for the administration of local government.* Would they all have teams and hold championships? Many, of course, like Notts and Cornwall, had old names covering old ground. Sides bearing such names were bound to continue, as though nothing had happened. But Cleveland, Avon, Merseyside had no such tradition. Moreover their people had other loyalties, to Durham, Gloucestershire, Lancashire etc. And if Humberside fielded sides, would North Yorks, for instance, do the same? For it too was a county, in exactly the same sense, whereas Yorkshire itself was not. If 'the Yorkshires' and Humberside each went their separate ways, it would be the end of sporting Yorkshire on its own. But even if it continued, how would it be defined?

Holding the Line. 'In Baulk' soon had reassuring news: *Barnoldswick clubs lead the way and will be 'saved' for Yorkshire snooker.* The Yorkshire Billiards Association had altered the rules to let 'transferred' players take part in its competitions and represent the County if selected. So clubs now in administrative Lancashire remained eligible for Yorkshire — a welcome step, helping to keep the changes within bounds. And it answered (or begged) other questions. Yes, Yorkshire would continue, but though the new Lancashire was 'for local government' it was likely to cover sport too. Wherever 'Yorkshire's' boundary was, it would not apparently overlap any part of 'Lancashire' — hence the word 'transferred'. West Craven had 'moved'..and had been restored for snooker..

There were, of course, snags. Players were not allowed two identities. When an Earby youth asked to play in both competitions Yorkshire said 'no'. He chose Lancs — because, said the Yorkshire secretary slyly, he thought he'd have a better chance there.

Several older sports, some famous, some obscure, followed the YBA. The Society of Archers, whose 'Antient Scorton (Richmond) Silver Arrow' has to be contested within Yorkshire's boundaries, made no change. In county cricket Yorkshire remained Yorkshire, not just 'the Yorkshires'; and the place you must have been born in to be qualified now included parts of a new Lancashire! The 150 clubs in the Yorkshire Golf Union still covered the land between Humber and Tees. (Its 1987 Yorkshire Championship was held at Redcar). Middlesbrough and Hull and East Riding went on playing in the Yorkshire Rugby Union competition. There were, after all, traditions to maintain — loyalties of clubs and people to each other — whatever their place might officially be; and they had never, usually, been beholden to county councils for money or anything else.

Compromise. But in tennis there was a different approach: the rules of the Yorkshire LTA were now expressed in terms of new counties, though 'Yorkshire' included 'North Humberside' while excluding south 'Cleveland'. Even so past links were respected. Those with a North Riding birth certificate were eligible for competitions and the county team; and the Middlesbrough (Linthorpe) club remained in membership.

The assumption here (echoed elsewhere) that Humberside was somehow more Yorkshire than Cleveland is interesting. Even so, the YLTA had to reckon with the County Council's desire for some form of separate participation in the sport — 'closed' Humberside competitions, for instance, and a separate county tennis agency falling short of full LTA status and not affecting membership of the Yorkshire LTA — to which local players and clubs remain loyal. Such were the muddled compromises arising from 1974, the unresolved clash between new politics and traditional identities. It was, meanwhile, a piquant fact that in the mid-1980s Yorkshire's annual competitions took place in Hull, on the most suitable site in the whole of Yorkshire — 28 grass courts, with 20 hard ones nearby for bad weather — and were sponsored by a Hull firm.

Eventually not even the sacred sport of cricket seemed wholly immune to change. At one stage a South Yorkshire County Club was mooted at Sheffield, though to no apparent effect; and in the Spring of 1986 a Councillor proposed the launching of a Humberside County Cricket Club, part of a plan to develop the ground where Yorkshire itself was wont to play, though too infrequently. A recently deposed Chairman of the YCCC, resident in Hull, saw no reason to withhold support; it would harm neither the Yorkshire club nor its East Yorkshire membership but would foster local talent, to everyone's benefit. And lest his own loyalties should seem in doubt he protested his White Rose credentials in extreme terms: *I will not even mention the name of 'Humberside' in my letterheads or in any other way. I am a Yorkshireman and an East Yorkshireman.* He was anxious only that youngsters should have good conditions to prepare them to play for their county...*which has been, and will remain, York-shire.* (Yorkshire Post correspondence. May 1986).

Confrontation. In athletics, meanwhile, co-existence grew difficult. The national AAA encouraged separate associations in the new counties — the divorce, therefore, of Humberside from Yorkshire (ie the Yorkshires). And a new association was treated as having always existed. Thus, even if you were born in East Riding days, in athletics it was to Humberside that you belonged. Only those who had already appeared for Yorkshire were exempt, and even they could opt for the new county.

Much as the AAA must have congratulated itself on its foresight — the rules were passed in advance of the county reforms — this was not a recipe for peace and quiet. The Yorkshire AAA, with old loyalties to maintain, having paid no attention to local government before, saw no reason to do so now. Its policy was 'no change'. On the whole it was what the athletes wanted. Humberside might send letters of complaint when 'their' people wanted to appear for Yorkshire or in the Yorkshire championships but some took no notice — Philip Cooke, for instance, a young star sprinter who ran for Yorkshire in 1985. By contrast, Dave Smith, a hammer-thrower born in Hull in East Riding days, represented Humberside in accordance with the rules...and won a gold medal. Confusion reigns. Epworth (Lincolnshire/Humberside) was never in Yorkshire but its mail was directed through Doncaster...and an Epworth youth appeared in the Yorkshire championships on that ground alone! A Yorkshire Post correspondent, noting that Lincolnshire could get in while Hull could not, concluded that Alice in Wonderland might as well run athletics.

An understandable view. If the AAA had treated Yorkshire as it continued to treat Middlesex, or if Humberside had decided, like all other new counties except Avon, to keep out, all would have been well. (No 'Greater Manchester' nor 'Merseyside' teams ever threatened the integrity of Lancashire or Cheshire in senior athletics). But far from keeping out, it used athletics to build identity. Its team turned out clad in yellow and black tracksuits and blazers paid for — like the coach transporting them — by the County Council itself.

Looking ahead. In future, it seemed, one thing more than any other might settle county identity through sport — local government control of schools. Three lines from the Craven Herald summed things up: *Earby's outstanding young cricketer .... made his debut for Lancashire's U13 side on Sunday. The 12 year-old.....was playing at Barrow against Cumbria. Yesterday he joined the side again at Radcliffe for a match against Humberside.*

Lancashire, Cumbria, Humberside. The boy was twelve, born in the year of reorganisation, unaware of a time when his hometown was not in 'Lancashire' (or when Barrow was), of a time when Cumbria and Humberside did not exist (or of the confusing fact that the home game was being played in a town in 'Greater Manchester', not in the 'Lancashire' that runs his school). He would find nothing incongruous in the line 'Lancashire, Cumbria, Humberside': the first name might be as new and artificial as the last two. And his generation might come to see nothing odd about it in senior sport either. Indeed, what could well appear strange is the idea of a Humberside boy, or man, playing for any other county — including Yorkshire.......were it not that there were still names in sport which were of place, not politics, the old names of the leagues where people played when they left school. In the mid nineteen-eighties playing cricket for Hull still meant playing in the Yorkshire League. Hornsea, Beverley and Bridlington were among seven Humberside clubs in the 'East Yorkshire Cup'. The league which Middlesbrough played in had only one 'North Yorkshire' side: the majority were in Cleveland. But it was still called the North Yorkshire/South Durham League. Such are the identities people stick to when the choice is theirs. Unwelcome ones are sent from above.

Yorkshire on the Page

Holy Scripture. Old family Bibles, too heavy to be held in the hands, are supportable only on one's knee, a table, a lectern. On a similar scale are four volumes published in the 1870s, written by Thomas Baines, MP for Leeds. Between thick, cloth-covered boards embossed with the crests of Yorkshire's great cities, they contain fine engravings of its bearded leaders — Salt, Crossley and the like, Old Testament patriarchs in waistcoats and watchchains. The biblical comparison is no accident. These mighty tomes, quite apart from what their gilt-edged pages say in words, were intended by their look and feel to convey the high majesty of their subject. Here, among all the transitory themes of mankind, is one which, like that of the Bible, is eternal: 'Yorkshire Past and Present: A History and a Description of the three Ridings of the Great County of York from the Earliest Ages to the year 1870'.

1870. Just over one hundred years later there occurred an event of which Encyclopaedia Britannica (1986), with all the authority of a 20th Century 'Bible', had this to say: *Yorkshire and the Ridings passed out of existence with the administrative reorganisation of 1974.*

Death. *Passed out of existence.* A solemn judgement, and seemingly a final one. It represented the new challenge faced by the literary community. Which Yorkshire, if any, could writers and publishers now acknowledge — the County of York, or 'the Yorkshires', or some other? If their subject was historical the answer was clearly the first of these, assuming, that is, that the story to be told ended in 1974. But time does not stand still, and Singleton and Rawnsley's 'A History of Yorkshire' (Phillimore 1986) takes us beyond that year, uses the word 'county' with the present tense, and concludes with an administrative analysis showing 'North Humberside' as well as 'the Yorkshires'. Maybe the history of our place had not, after all, come to an end. If you wished to write on other topics — 'Yorkshire Craftsmen at Work', for instance, or Yorkshire architecture — you had to set bounds to your subject: must you leave out Saltburn and Hornsea, Beverley and Middlesbrough? Should the Reports of the Yorkshire Philosophical Society no longer list lectures on 'Humberside' themes? There was also the collection of knowledge to think of, long a function of county geography. How would the naturalists now group their records, or the archaeologists?

And what about the revision of works already written? William Smith's 'Old Yorkshire' (1881-1885) included no fewer than 50 Yorkshire subjects, from Abbeys to Artists, Poets to Peerages, Songs to Superstitions, each theme pre-fixed with the County's name. While no one, perhaps, would ever wish to update such a work, that was not true of others — of Pevsner's famous 'The Buildings of England', for instance. Would his 'Yorkshire, the North Riding' (Penguin 1966) have to be aligned with new political areas when reissued? If so, it was a pity that the date of publication had not been ten years later. But Pevsner would not have been around by then. And there seemed, in any case, insufficient reason for such a change. Like other counties, that of York had been the geographical basis for countless books, on almost every kind of topic. Ironically, one subject rarely if ever the chosen theme, and receiving scarcely a mention even in histories, was local government. Could a change in that alone really cause literature in general to alter course?

Resurrection. Since 1974 the authors themselves have had little doubt what they wanted to write about. Even Encyclopaedia Britannica, having consigned Yorkshire to oblivion, in the very same year revealed, in its own sister publication, Macropaedia, that a place with that name was still to be found; and that it even included land outside 'the Yorkshires'. *Yorkshire is not only industry – there are extensive areas of farming, the deep-sea fishing industry[2] operating from Hull, and tourist country along a fine coast.*

It was a common approach: *The region covered,* (R. A. Carter in 'A Visitor's Guide to Yorkshire Churches', Watmoughs, 1976) *is that of the real Yorkshire. Although the new county designations are used, churches are included which some now consider to be in Durham, Cumbria and even Lancashire.*

The county which lies in the hearts and minds of most Yorkshire people, and which existed on the map for the millenium before the boundary changes of 1974 has not changed. (Singleton and Rawnsley, op.cit.).

Such famous places as Hull, Bridlington, Beverley and Middlesbrough (Ward Lock's 'Yorkshire', reprinted 1982) *are Yorkshire to the core. It would be perverse to exclude them from such a Guide as this.*

The Yorkshire Coastline in Sketches', by C. Milner (Hutton 1986) covers the coast from Tees to Spurn. *It is,* claims the author, *the coastline of its true identity since all who live along it consider themselves Yorkshire folk.*

Meanwhile writers like R. W. Morris ('Yorkshire through Place-names', David and Charles 1982) found practical reasons for their choice. He had based his book on the County of York because 'the bulk of the information is grouped according to the three Ridings'. The Yorkshire Archaeological Society, for its part, neither adopted the unlovely title 'Yorkshire and Humberside' nor yet sought to exclude from its Journal (see 1984 edition) articles on the Skipsea area, the Percy Tomb (Beverley Minster) and 'A Bronze Object found at Brough-on-Humber'. Any change in its policy would involve re-cataloguing 30,000 books and would serve little purpose. J. R. Mather, ('Birds of Yorkshire' Croom Helm 1986) saw no reason to depart from the boundaries used by his predecessors on the same subject, Nelson (1907) and Chislett (1952).

Nor were the Yorkshire authors alone in writing about familiar places. 'The

Architecture of England' (Macmillan 1986) appeared in two volumes, northern and southern. Its authors, John Julius Norwich and John Martin Robinson, noted the chaotic state of the literature and the records, accused bureaucrats of 'riding roughshod over English history', sympathised with those having to live in *previously unheard-of areas – I would not presume to compare my irritation with theirs* — and proceeded to divide the land as best they could. They acknowledged no Humberside or Cleveland, but East Yorkshire and a North Yorkshire that not only includes Yarm but *contains all that is most marvellous in our landscape.* (Even a Yorkshireman must enquire whether they had forgotten the Lake District). As for the whole thing, it exists and is a county. *Yorkshire is the heart of the North and the largest English county. It is also the most richly endowed architecturally as it contains the biggest and best of everything.*

Misgivings. Even so, a sense of contradiction and confusion was abroad. Like the Encyclopaedia Britannica, the Yorkshire Annual 1975 put things both ways: *Yorkshire as a County is no more* and *Technically there is now no such species as a Yorkshireman (or woman)* ...but... the Annual's aim was to have appeal for *Yorkshire folk everywhere – including those exiled.* (So the 'race' had, after all, survived, and had somewhere to be exiled from). In 1981 an anthology called 'Yorkshire Pride' (produced, like the Annual, by The Dalesman) placed today's indefinite concept — *Yorkshire is vast and varied* — alongside a precision which belonged, apparently, only to yesterday — *before 1974 Yorkshire had 3,906,940 acres.* But it included also a Yorkshire Ridings Society statement ('The Real Yorkshire') to the effect that yesterday and today were the same: only the county councils, not the Ridings, had changed.

The Place without a Number. As we have seen, post-1974 writers often write as though that were true. What they have not felt able to do is to say that it is. Morris, instead, speaks of 'former' Ridings, Willis[3] of 'old' boundaries. For Pill everything is over — *no longer are there three Ridings* — despite his book's title ('Yorkshire: the West biding' Batsford 1977). The author of 'The Yorkshire Coast in Sketches', having espoused *its true identity,* recants somewhat with yesterday's adverb: *this part of Britain will always be nostalgically known as the Yorkshire coast.* Most understandably, considering what has happened to maps, John Rawnsley's fine 'Antique Maps of Yorkshire and their Makers' (3rd Edition, pub J. M. Rigg 1983), records *a more drastic change than any recorded in recent centuries.....at the stroke of a pen..... Yorkshire ceased to exist.*

Such grim talk might even have sprung partly from changes peculiar to the book-trade itself. For the latest version of the Dewey numerical code used to classify books by subject no longer included the Ridings of Yorkshire: they had been replaced by the new names. Nor did 'Yorkshire' (singular) appear. The rule was that anything written on that 'redundant' topic had to be given a 'West Yorkshire' number. This could have perplexing consequences. A book called 'Shipwrecks off the Yorkshire Coast' obviously could not be given the code of an area without a coastline, whatever the rule said. So it was listed twice, under 'North Yorkshire' and 'Humberside'. (Why not 'Cleveland', as well?)

Meanwhile the place without so much as a number to call its own had, in a period of twelve years since 1974, been the named subject of far more books than all its coded counterfeits put together.

That being so, a question arose: if the County of York was what writers, including non-historians, wished to write about, why were they so diffident about it? If a book about the Yorkshire coast was indeed about that, and if its Bridlington printer and Beverley publisher both gave their present address as East Yorkshire, why say that the coast's name is 'nostalgically' Yorkshire? If writers on architecture wished to ignore Humberside and Cleveland why did they not organise their work under the Ridings and have done?

And right on cue, there appeared, in 1987, 'The Yorkshire Ridings' (Tookey and Morgan, pub Fraser). At last no gloom or apology. *All Yorkshire, the Yorkshire of the three Ridings, is the subject of this book. It is* — present tense — *of course the biggest county in England and huge in the variety of its landscapes.*

Yorkshire in the Market

The Goods. In the late 1980s a supposedly defunct concept flourished in trade and commerce. A thriving Bank, a Building Society and now even a Unit Trust — sure symbol of the Thatcher years — bore the name. Others might wonder what, where and even whether Yorkshire was: the Trust evidently knew, its policy being to invest in 'Yorkshire-based' companies....which had, in fact, being doing well *thanks to their prudent financial controls* — a euphemism for parsimony? — *for which Yorkshire people are renowned.*

The name's commercial cachet was evident elsewhere. *Direct Windows – made by Yorkshiremen in Yorkshire for Yorkshire homes* ran the advert on the side of a Leeds bus. *Choose Yorkshire Pride,* sang another manufacturer, *and you are choosing all that's fine in Yorkshire craftsmanship ....It's a well-known fact that the people of Yorkshire expect real value.* (Tightness again?) They were giving value too. *Building workers from Yorkshire bring a level of craftsmanship which their* (London) *employers say cannot be had from London tradesmen.* (The Times, on a Sheffield group commuting to the capital to build flats).

The idea seemed to go with a sense of wholesomeness drawn from continuity with the past: *Old-fashioned Yorkshire Biscuits from the village of Haworth, Yorkshire...combine tradition, original recipes and the finest natural ingredients with Yorkshire pride.* The livery-clad figure on the wrapper of a product made in Berkshire did not speak with a Berkshire accent: *Bread wi' nowt taken out.* Not that Yorkshiremen lived by bread alone — not even, you might say, by Whitbread. For many brewers, too, went on exploiting pride of place and pride in their past: Theakston's 'Old Peculiar Yorkshire Ale'; Webster's and Bentley's 'Yorkshire Bitter'; Whitbread's 'Yorkshire Brewed Ales'; the products of the Smiths, Samuel and John, of Tadcaster, the County's brewing capital: *Beer brewed in Yorkshire's Oldest Brewery* (Samuel's. Founded 1758). Tetley's management, spurred by evident patriotism as well as commerce, lost no chance to support the County of York — and to get customers to do the same with their car stickers: *Yorkshire's Right Champion; Yorkshire Born and Brewed.*

Some goods are what they seem, others are not. *Best Yorkshire Red Potatoes* ran the advert in a Bedfordshire paper (for beer is not the only thing that sells well 'abroad'). *Grown on limestone,* it added, for reassurance. And you might have thought that another product, 'Yorkshire Pot Holes', had something to do with limestone too ... until you read the small print: *The wooden toilet seat has served us well over the years* (tradition again) *with its superior warmth, comfort and durability.*

The Market. What is the Yorkshire of trade and commerce? What place were advertisers referring to? The Yorkshire General Unit Trust had to be clear about this, since it was pledged to put at least 75% of its investment into 'Yorkshire' companies; and it used 'broadly' the area of the three Ridings. Other organisations did not say what they meant; nor did they need to. Without definition the term suggested size — a large market — tradition, quality... and that was enough.

Nevertheless it was used more often in some places than others. Enter Leeds at the west end of the urban motorway and there was no doubting where you were: *one of Yorkshire's oldest fitting stations* (car exhausts) on one side, with the 'Yorkshire Post' tower ahead, telling you the time and temperature; and on the other a sign pointing to 'Yorkshire Chemicals plc' and the YTV building looming in the middle distance. In Sheffield Yorkshire did not obtrude so. But it never had. In the late sixties only eight organisations had had a 'Yorkshire' name and a Sheffield telephone number: in Leeds there were 52. Twenty years later the comparison was 19 and 71. The same is true of Hull and Middlesbrough as of Sheffield. It has more to do with location than local government. From Leeds — and Bradford and York, where commercial 'Yorkshire' also looms large — journeys through the County radiate in all directions. Places on the edge feel different. Little wonder that Middlesbrough — 56 'Cleveland' telephone entries by 1984 — should capitalise on the area whose central focus it is, or that in the Hull Directory, while 'Yorkshire/East Riding' entries remained steady at about 16, 'Humber/Humberside' had multiplied many times since 1974 to over 50.

Yorkshire in the media

"Wider still and wider". But the Yorkshire of commerce (and culture) now had an ally which dwarfed the rest and sent an old word far beyond old boundaries. Yorkshire Television, advertising a place as well as consumer goods, day and night caused millions to hear and see the name (and to listen to its — probably unrecognised — five-note 'Ilkla Moor' jingle). Has any British place-name ever had a more constant airing? *Yorkshire Television Ltd.* ran its sale of shares brochure. *is the company which provides the television programmes in Yorkshire.* Fair enough. And what did *in Yorkshire* mean? A region, not a county — one whose bounds were set, not by mankind but by radio physics — the location and power of its two main transmitters. And since one of these was in the middle of Lincolnshire, no wonder the accompanying map looked strange. Here was a 'Yorkshire' whose northern edge excluded Swaledale while its southern one embraced King's Lynn and other parts of East Anglia. Strange or not, its outline was witnessed daily in association with a name once used to label three Ridings. It is a far cry from the Vikings to UHFs. Our old place was made by the Danes, this new one by electronics. And what an area, what a people. 6 million of them! Roy Hattersley wrote that Yorkshire only now existed as the name of a cricket team. He was forgetting the TV Company.

Images. The visual media did more than publicise a name: they brought life to the idea. In its day the impact of Willie Riley's novel, 'Windyridge' — 300,000 copies sold from publication in 1912 — was legend, the peacefulness of his Yorkshire moorland cottage so coveted by hundreds of readers that they appropriated the name for their own dwelling, cottage or no. Thereafter the succession of 20C best-sellers with Yorkshire themes and authorship[4] was remarkable, from Priestley, Phyllis Bentley ('Inheritance', 1932, reprinted 29 times), Winifred Holtby ('South Riding', 1936) and Thomas Armstrong ('The Crowthers of Bankdam', 1940) to a group all publishing round about 1960, led by John Braine (Room at the Top), and including Stan Barstow (A Kind of Loving), David Storey (This Sporting Life) and Keith Waterhouse (Billy Liar) — the latter group heralded, as it were, by Richard Hoggart's influential portrayal of working-class life in Hunslet (The Uses of Literacy 1957). All these, except the last, were adapted for the screen and together with screenplays like those of Alan Bennett (eg 'A Private Function') with Alan Plater (The Beiderbecke Tapes) provided huge audiences with a varied experience of the Yorkshire scene. And if the resulting image might seem weighted towards the urban and even the sordid the balance was surely restored by three popular television series of the 1970s and 80s — firm weekly fixtures in the viewing diaries of millions: the comic knockabout of 'Last of the Summer Wine', set in the marvellous (and previously little known) Pennine countryside near Holmfirth; the long-running 'Emmerdale Farm', a gentle portrayal of life in the rural West Riding; and 'All Creatures Great and Small', Herriot's stories of a vet's encounters with the formidable denizens, animal and human, of North Riding dales and moorland. As a result new geographical names — 'Herriot Country' and even 'Last of the Summer Wine Country' — arrived to change the prospects of hoteliers, boarding house proprietors and coach tour operators alike, much as the 19th Century work of three young sisters, (some of it, too, filmed), turned Haworth, alas, into 'Bronteland'.

Words. Even if its impact is weaker, the printed word outstays the visual image; and the press was mostly faithful to the county's integrity. Through the 'eighties Yorkshire Life, The Dalesman, Yorkshire Topic as readily featured Hornsea as Hawes...and without apology or explanation. Yorkshire Ridings Magazine, with an office in Driffield, flaunted a Yorkshire address. Though 'Yorkshire's National Newspaper' has a reputation for putting first things first (*Yorkshireman in Watching Crowd as Thousands Perish*), it did not usually, apart from leaders supporting the Countrywomen's Association and the Yarm campaigners, tackle identity head-on. Instead a kind of unofficial truce operated. The Post meekly showed new maps, boundaries, names. But there was a 'Hull and East Riding Edition' and a 'Dining in the Ridings' feature — with North, South, West...and East Yorkshire sections. Its Calendar included East Yorkshire scenes; its annual 'Yorkshire Guide' was 'one of the best yet to the Ridings'. The footballing fortunes of Middlesbrough and Hull City were reported as Yorkshire concerns.

There was even the odd sign of territorial aggrandisement.... or unconscious error. If Humberside existed, it was in Yorkshire — all of it. Thus, the Post could report the threat of an MP to resign *if a nuclear dump was set up in Yorkshire,* while the accompanying map showed the place, South Killingholme, to be south of the Humber. Similarly the YEP: *The league table for cold spots in Yorkshire last night is Humberside, minus 13C, Harrogate, minus 12.5C* and so on: but 'Humberside' here meant the airport at Kirmington, between Grimsby and Scunthorpe. More seriously, mistakes could work in the other direction, and in contexts where it mattered. The YEP's excellent 'Restore the Ridings' edition not only described Dent (West Riding) as a former North Riding place but lamented the banishment of Stokesley — *what a beauty spot we lost* — to Cleveland. Even if the false premiss (Yorkshire = 'the Yorkshires') were true, Stokesley (North Yorkshire) was never 'lost'.

Yorkshire in Focus: Yorkshire Society (1980)

The concern of a Society founded in 1980, however, was not with boundaries. It aimed rather at obtaining *a better deal for Yorkshire.* Its founding Chairman, Mr. David Daniel, explained: *There's an underlying pride in the people of Yorkshire, but they're not very good at promoting the County in an organised way. Almost the only things on a Yorkshire scale are the Great Yorkshire Show and the County Cricket Club.* It was important to establish other things in the name of the County as a whole; and Mr Daniel confirmed that 'County' included Saddleworth, as though of all remote places that one could best point the definition.

The Yorkshire Society (1980) acquired distinguished Vice-Presidents — including Lord Wilson of Rievaulx — and an ambitious set of objectives: improving Yorkshire amenities through local branches, helping with efforts to promote tourism and to ease unemployment, getting people together in fellowship, fund-raising for special projects. Within a short period it had useful achievements to record. An annual Yorkshire History Prize, funded by a West Yorkshire County Council grant, administered through the Edward Boyle Memorial Trust and adjudicated by academics from the County's universities, was first presented in 1987. Wall plaques commemorating eminent Yorkshire people were mounted with appropriate ceremonial and the cooperation of local authorities and business firms, at Tingley (Christopher Saxton), Skipton (Thomas Spencer, of Marks and Spencer), Halifax (Percy Shaw, inventor of 'cats-eyes') and Kirkstall (Colonel North, presenter of the Abbey grounds to the City of Leeds and Yorkshire). Representations were made on public issues like the need to improve air transport services by the extension of flying hours at Leeds/Bradford airport. There were educational talks and visits, links were forged with Yorkshire Societies throughout the UK and steps taken to revive the London Society.

Eight years on, the Society's goals, a measure of the enthusiasm of Mr.

Community Health Council

East Yorkshire Health Authority

"Wider still..." The Yorkshire Television region.

On Wakefield station – patriotic ambiguity.

Daniel and his co-Founder, the Secretary, Mr. Barry Whittaker, remained a formidable challenge to the mainly West Riding-based group. Not that there was any doubting their validity. For whether the emphasis was on the geographical (as in the Ridings Society) or on the social and cultural side, Yorkshire's interests needed strong voices which, given its fragmented state in local government, it was unlikely to get from that source.

In 1985 the Society inaugurated an annual Yorkshire Day Civic Parade at York. The invitation list included almost 200 VIPs: MPs, Lords Lieutenant, High Sheriffs, Peers of the Realm, Lord Mayors and Chairmen of Town and District Councils. The attendance, and the occasion, were gratifying.

But there was a flaw. The invitation list being based on modern local government, the whole of Humberside was invited, including North Lincolnshire: and people from Grimsby and Barton-on-Humber came — to celebrate the Day of Yorkshire's Integrity. Nothing wrong with that perhaps. But equally, parts of Yorkshire were left out. No invitation went to Saddleworth, Sedbergh, West Craven, Middlesbrough.

By 1987, this omission having been repaired for the Wakefield ceremony, it was observed that Saddleworth's reply used notepaper bearing a crest with the words 'Saddleworth Parish Council: in the County of York'. And on the day, its ceremonial badge of office was seen to feature one symbol only, the White Rose itself.

Yorkshire in the Big Time

In the mid-80s, then, Yorkshire was a complex notion. In politics 'the Yorkshires' covered much of it, but not all, and the County of York, and even its Ridings, showed many signs of continuing life, mainly, though not wholly, outside local government. But to complicate matters further, the idea had another ingredient, the Region.

There had always been something strange about regarding as one county a place which actually had more than one inside it. It was the mysterious mathematics of religion: three in one and one in three. And the mystery was all the deeper in that one of the three on its own, the West Riding, was greater in area than any other in the country, with the North Riding not far behind. As for population, in County Cricket, though Yorkshire's birth qualification was a natural source of pride, it had to be conceded that with a ninth of England's manhood to draw on a county ought to be able to manage against the others — as indeed it had, and more, until they called in the help of the former British Empire!

Here, then, was not a typical county, but something intermediate, between county and nation — and conveniently so, for many were the services, products, organisations, which required such a basis for dealing with England. The 40 counties were too many, and varied too much in size: the country as a whole was too big. So, from Labour Party to Baptist Union, from Independent Television to Water Authorities, from Cancer Research Appeals to National Trust, they had divided England up. Among public authorities the number of regions varied : Economic Planning had 8, Sport and Recreation 9, Electricity

11, Arts 12, Health 14. There were 10 areas for water and gas. But whatever the number, Yorkshire was always one, and, except for the Gas Board ('North East') — (did they actually prefer that unlovely acronym NEGAS?) — its name was always used, often the only real name among them, the rest being mere compass points, 'North West', 'South East' etc (though sometimes the approach was more romantic, with 'Northumbria', 'Wessex' etc).

Not that 'Yorkshire' was always alone. Entering this league it had left all other counties behind..... with one exception. For 'Yorkshire and Humberside' was sometimes used to denote the Region, depending mainly on the area covered. In particular it was the name given to one of eight 'Standard Regions of England', used by the Registrar General for population censuses. Traditionalists, of course, resented the second half because it seemed to endorse the 1974 interloper. It is worth noting, however, that the Standard Region had had exactly the same name before the new county arrived... when the latter half was presumably there to denote the riverbank part of Lincolnshire. (And even traditionalists might reflect that progress is not always backwards: before 1974 the North Riding had not been in the 'Yorkshire and Humberside' of census-takers and economic planners at all — now all three 'Yorkshires' were in).

The big league mattered to identity, in two ways. First, here already were organisations, some of them large public authorities, showing by their names and areas that Yorkshire existed and that it was not merely 'the Yorkshires': Yorkshire Water, for instance, the YEB and the Regional Health Authority might cover different, overlapping ground, but they all included 'North Humberside'. But in the longer run the English regions might be destined for even bigger things. There was always life outside politics; but there might be new life inside too.

Devolution. In 1977 a conference in Denmark on 'Europe of the Regions', attended by people from historic communities like Flanders, Normandy, Catalonia, Tyrol, Wessex, Scotland and Wales, was informed that Britain was *centralised to the point of lunacy.* (The speaker, Northcote Parkinson, of Parkinson's Law fame, had, as it happens, been reared in York).

The thought was already familiar. In the sixties Scottish and Welsh nationalists had begun to thrive on Britain's poor economic performance and sense of relative decline. There must, it seemed, be more effective ways of running a nation of over 50 million souls. If Norway (population 4 million) and Denmark (5 million) were large enough to be wholly self-governing, should not Scotland, with a population like Denmark's, have a measure of independence? And were there not parts of England with the size, coherence and sense of identity to justify similar arrangements?

The MP for Normanton felt sure he could think of one. It had 5 million people. *Yorkshire*, said Mr. Roberts, *is completely viable and self-supporting with a wide diversity of industries.* He would be asking the Environment Secretary — it was the occasion of the 1971 White Paper — for similar status to Northern Ireland, a Parliament, local taxes and perhaps full-time MPs. The YEP waxed mock chauvinistic. *UDI for Yorks!...Territorial take-over by Tykes. Yorkshire folk, as everyone knows, have all the virtues of a perfect race and already regard themselves as independence personified..It is doubtful if any other region has such a wide variety of industry and commerce, and production figures...compare with the best. It's a fact that if we refused to 'export' our clothing, most of the country would end up half-naked. Yorkshire's mills supply the whole world.* The rapturous chronicle embraced coal production, steel, chemicals and electricity, with brewing, fisheries and agriculture thrown in. Output was shown to be a high proportion of the national totals.

The basic idea was not new. Two years earlier, after the most extensive local government survey ever made, the 'Maud Report' had proposed a Yorkshire Province, one of eight in England. Earlier still, in 1966, the Yorkshire Post had reported a 9 Region plan by Tory MPs (Mr. Roberts was Labour) which included Yorkshire. And to complete the political scene, the Liberal Party, latterly with its Social Democratic allies, had long supported the devolution of political power. *Yorkshire ready for Assembly* ran the report on its local discussions with the YRS in 1978. *Contempt and alienation are engendered by policies which pay no regard to loyalties, identity and feelings.* Attention was drawn to two of the party's publications: 'A Parliament for Yorkshire' (1976) and 'Devolution: the Yorkshire Dimension' (1977).

Ten years later regional government and the reinforcement of identity it could bring was no nearer. Labour had buried Maud's proposal in 1970 and no one had urged its revival. Furthermore, only a decade after Mr. Roberts's suggestions, the economic power used to support them had mostly disappeared. Fisheries and textiles, steel and coal mining, had dwindled. The case for 'independence' would now have to rest more on defending the weak than on exploiting strength. (It is, of course, legitimate — if fruitless — to ponder whether things would not have been different in a Yorkshire Province).

Names and areas. If the idea were ever to be made a reality what land, what names, would appear on new political maps? Would historic Yorkshire be respected? It seems unlikely. True, the Tory MPs had used the Ridings, with Leeds as regional capital, and Middlesbrough as county capital of the North Riding — probably the last proposal explicitly to include Middlesbrough in administrative Yorkshire. Maud, however, had given Teesside to 'the North', had included in its Yorkshire Province part of Lindsey, referred to as 'South Humberside'....and had thereby drawn criticism from one who, after a distinguished local government career, still had a feel for history and sentiment: *It would be fundamentally wrong to associate part of Lindsey with Yorkshire ....Lindsey belongs to Lincolnshire and it would be wholly dominated by association with Yorkshire and would be virtually disenfranchised.* ....the views of Sir Bernard Kenyon, former Clerk to the West Riding County Council and firm believer in 'one Yorkshire'.

The regional idea implies, of course, a difficult notion — that of a single area for various agencies which, in the late 1980s, covered different ones. The writ of the Health Authority did not run in Sheffield or Barnsley, while 'Yorkshire Arts' did not look after Hull. 'Yorkshire Water' came nearest to covering the whole County: it was the elemental geography of the first Viking boatmen —

the catchment basin of the Ouse, together with the North Riding Esk and East Riding Hull — that determined its territory.

The Ridings Society, as might be expected, had no doubt which ground and title, if any, should enter the big league of politics: *Throughout this document 'Yorkshire' means the geographical county of the East, West and North Ridings together with York, and not an aggregation of local authorities which happen to have 'Yorkshire' in their names.* ('What Future for Yorkshire?' (1977)). As for a capital, the claims of Leeds and Sheffield could be ignored. Nor, happily, need a neutral compromise — a Yorkshire Canberra or Brasilia — be specially built. A former seat of the Roman Emperor himself would surely serve: the City of York — *having the style and character of a governmental centre, and being outside the rivalry of the two largest Yorkshire cities.* Names other than Yorkshire were rejected, including 'the North' — a 'Campaign for the North' was in temporary vogue — and especially 'Yorkshire and Humberside', for it was essential that a provincial assembly had *an emotional as well as a rational appeal.*

By the later 1980s, however, that unhappy pairing was, in officialdom, coming to seem as inevitable as 'strawberries and cream'. To others it read more like 'strawberries and instant whip', except that the fruit itself, being 'the Yorkshires', not the real thing, was also a fake.

FOOTNOTES

[1] Though 'County of York' is used here and hereafter to denote the ancient place, the name 'Yorkshire' in its Anglo-Saxon form, 'Eoforwicscir', is earlier.

[2] A somewhat anachronistic claim, in 1986.

[3] R. Willis, 'Yorkshire's Historic Buildings' (Hale 1975).

[4] As many as 182 were invited to a dinner held exclusively for authors of Yorkshire birth/residence in 1938.

CHAPTER 9: VERDICT AND PROSPECT

Logic. Pears Encyclopaedia 1983 defined two great regions as follows:

Normandy, historic prov. of France; on English Channel; now divided into deps Manche, Calvados, Eure, Seine-maritime and part of Orne; Rouen was cap. Channel Is. were part of old Duchy; conquered England 1066; allied invasion of Europe 1944.

Yorkshire, former co., Eng., formerly divided into 3 separate admin. parts (Ridings) N.E. and W. now split into 3 non-met cos., Cleveland, North Yorks and Humberside and 2 met.cos. West Yorks and South Yorks.

'Historic' province — 'former' county. Normandy comes off better here; clearly a special word was needed for a place that had once conquered England. (Winning the County Cricket Championship hardly ranks with that). But in 1983 Normandy's administrative role was long over, was even more 'former' than Yorkshire's. *The concept of Normandy ought to have been destroyed,* wrote the authors of 'Portrait of Normandy' (Hale, 1974) *but it exists quite forcefully today. The Norman knows he is a Norman and prides himself on the fact.* It reminded them of a special English breed. *A Yorkshireman has the same geographical certainty and pride, but Yorkshire is still a geographical and political, maybe an ethnic entity.....mediaeval divisions still hold sway in men's hearts.*

The English tourist does not need reminding that Normandy is still alive. Yet its 'abolition' occurred 2 centuries ago. 'Life after politics' indeed. There is hope for Yorkshire yet.

But what was that about 'geographical certainty'? The words were written before the English reforms and their confusing aftermath. Which Yorkshire will survive — 'the Yorkshires', the Region, or the County of York....or a mixture of the three? If the answer is uncertain it is surely because 1974 mostly tried to hi-jack place-loyalty for political purposes while leaving some places out, including many Yorkshire places. With characteristic logic the French kept separate things separate; (indeed the revolutionaries may have wanted to stamp out the past altogether. If so they failed) and Normandy lives without the dubious help of some of its 'départements' bearing its own name while others do not. *Perhaps* wrote a perceptive Yorkshireman to the press *the worst mistake was to give the new authorities 'Yorkshire' names and boundaries similar to the old ones.* Perhaps indeed. In France all the names were new, but though the average Englishman will be hard pressed to recall many of them, in local government they will be none the worse for that. And the identity of the great French provinces continues undisturbed.

Confusion. The reformers in England were, of course, right about one thing — the loyalty of English people to their counties. But the idea that county government itself was the object of such feelings was mistaken, and so were two related beliefs: that local government needed place-loyalty in order to function effectively, and that counties could not survive as places without a political role. You could hear the muddle developing as the reforms emerged: *If we can keep the loyalties that exist in counties,* the Minister had said, introducing them, *that may be an overall advantage.* And he chided the opposition for its perfidy: *Under the proposals of the Gentlemen opposite only Notts and Shropshire would have remained* (an assertion belied by the persistence of Middlesex, the counties of Scotland and Northern Ireland, and indeed Yorkshire). He was accepting the kind of argument put to the Royal Commission by Herefordshire — that councils needed historical and cultural roots; *it is true that county councils in their present form are of comparatively recent origin, but county government had been exercised for hundreds of years before 1888, and the fact of being, for instance, a Yorkshire Man* (sic) *is usually a proud boast*[1]. Indeed it was, and is. But what had that to do with administration? And how important was the principle anyway? Would it apply everywhere? No, there would be 'rootless' new counties even in the ancient place used by Herefordshire to support its argument.

It is easy, indeed, to set up a council and give it an area to manage, but you cannot create a place like that. Yorkshire and, for instance, Somerset have presented images — of landscape and weather, towns and villages, ways of speech, architecture, people living and dead; in a word, home. And a system in which many old concepts like those two were joined by a few new ones meant trouble for the latter.

Unfinished business. In a 1978 (7 July) Leader article, the Times saw English local government as a problem still awaiting a solution: counties like Avon and Humberside, it said, were seen as artificial and offensive to tradition; most counties were the wrong size anyway to provide efficient services — too large for some purposes, too small for others; if it became possible to replace the county with a more appropriate pattern, Somerset, Cumberland, Rutland and the rest should have their historic identity officially restored. And how would this be done? The Leader did not say. Never mind. If the Thunderer said it should, then it certainly could[2].

For the problem remains, years after that was written — the result of a failure either to endorse the historic counties as a whole or to make the distinctions that would have left local government free to do its primary job. The reforms trifled with place-loyalty, as a desirable, but optional extra, instead of starting from it, or leaving it alone. The Boundary Commission was to note the effects, in the County of York and elsewhere. *I don't like Humberside,* a young man told me, himself an employee of the County Council: *It's a bit like being occupied by the Germans* ....and he wasn't smiling. The 'Back to Somerset' file in Bristol Library is inches thick, and the tone of letters to the Bath Guardian dire and forlorn: *We don't belong to Avon, we belong to Somerset....We loathe Avon. It is like a rude four-letter word to most people in the village....We were born and bred in Somerset and don't want to be anywhere else....No longer can we be part of that 'smiling Somerset' of history and legend.* No doubt the chagrin of 'Avon' people is the deeper for seeing that others, a few miles away, still live under their old name. (At least Westmorland was spared that). New authorities, meanwhile, had a hard enough job simply to provide efficient services; they should surely not have had an extra task inadvertently thrust upon them — and impossible in any case — that of creating a socio-cultural place, embodying all that the East Riding, Lincolnshire, Gloucestershire and Somerset had meant. The dispiriting effect on the members and officers of Avon County Council — no less able and hard-working than their counterparts elsewhere — of polls like the one in Weston-Super-Mare in 1982 can only be imagined. 62% voted — a staggering number, and in a poll organised and paid for by private citizens — and of these, 98.6% supported a 'Return to Somerset'. There were similar results in the nearby villages. But it was not just — indeed not mainly — about 'services': they wanted their home back.

They are unlikely ever to get it. A Parliament which was not sensitive enough to stop the Post Office imposing new addresses in 1974 will surely never restore it to them. Yet even that small measure would almost certainly have drawn the sting of much discontent, in Somerset and in the Ridings as well. It would have made local government reform seem less blatantly undemocratic.

The Commission speaks. For that is exactly what it has seemed. Before 1974, people in the East Riding, in Lincolnshire and in Somerset had voted by huge majorities (85% in Somerset) against change, when given the rare chance to express a view. Their wishes were ignored. Ten years later opposition had, if anything, intensified (see Ch.6 North Lincolnshire Association) so that even the Boundary Commission, in its draft verdict on the review of Humberside (June 1987), felt moved to write: *there must come a point at which long-standing and strongly held feelings of alienation towards an authority on the part of large numbers of its residents will in themselves call for a re-examination of the justification for its existence, at least in its present form.* Predictably, however, that point had not yet, in the Commission's view, been reached. Equally predictable was its interim response on the boundaries of Cumbria and North Yorkshire. At Sedbergh it noted *the depth of feeling shown by people who wished to return to the county to which they belonged before local government reorganis- ation* but felt unable to agree. In the North Riding the appeals from Yarm, Loftus and Guisborough were similarly brushed aside. The Commission's report described the referenda as 'opinion polls' and did not even quote the figures. A figure it did mention came from a surprising source — that forgotten Yorkshire land of the upper Tees (Map 11) where the parish of Boldron and Ovington had voted 78% in favour of transfer from Durham to North York- shire: but to no avail. Of the 'North Yorkshire' movement in West Craven the report managed to state, within a dozen lines, both that it had secured 1308 signatures and that it had attracted 'little support'. The Commission, no doubt

Map 11. The Upper Tees and Stainmore.

with some justice, considered that the motivation of those seeking transfer had less to do with local government than with *the strongly held feelings of loyalty towards the old county of Yorkshire.* In other words it was due to muddle. But the muddle was not of the people's making. The system seemed to offer only one way of recovering their familiar place.

In one place only — small, but famous in the catalogue of Yorkshire superlatives — was the people's wish heard. At the landlord's request, Tan Hill, 'the highest pub in England', was to pass from Durham to North Yorkshire. (Map 11).

Yorkshire: reading the tea leaves. Small hope, then, for those who might wish to see the real Yorkshire's boundaries expressed in politics one day: even 'the Yorkshires' were not to be extended by more than a few acres. But there are other reasons for pessimism about a political County of York — whether as a group of districts and counties or as a 'region/province' within some new national order. Given that local government reform is a 'top-down' affair, much depends on those with access to Westminster. And most are simply uninterested. *Who speaks for Yorkshire?* asked the YEP in 1971. The answer was non-political John Fisher and his little group. Marcus Fox helped Great Ayton and Whitby; Albert Roberts dreamed his dream; the rest was silence. When, in 1979, all General Election candidates in Yorkshire and Lincolnshire were asked about their commitment to traditional county names and areas, all but a few

129

gave assurances....with no perceptible result. Social Democrats were welcomed to their 1986 Conference by the local (Harrogate) candidate with the statement that *the loss of the Ridings is unacceptable to the people of Yorkshire;* but the topic was not on the Conference Agenda. While Liberals express outrage at historic Yorkshire's dismemberment their so-called 'Yorkshire Alliance' is a post-1974 affair and their Yorkshire parliament booklets are out of print. In fact, if ever there was capital to be made of the feelings that undoubtedly go with the County of York, no politician has tried seriously to make any. It is not clear that they should have: it is clear that they have not.

Nor has there ever been much unity within Yorkshire in promoting it. The Yorkshire Society are right about that. The various pressure groups have usually acted independently. If the 'Back to Yorkshire' movements were about local government, they were rightly seen as a local matter; if they were about 'belonging to Yorkshire' they concerned the rest of Yorkshire....which, however, did not even know about them. The YEP's campaign was indeed its own and no-one else's. The City of Leeds changed its address without calling on other authorities to do the same. (Perhaps it recalled a leading role it once undertook in the County's name, the founding of the ill-fated Yorkshire Symphony Orchestra (1946) amid the idealism and optimism of the post-war period, the participation at first of many Yorkshire authorities, including Hull — but not Sheffield and Bradford, both wedded to the Halle — the gradual waning of audiences and funds...and eventual failure in 1955). Socially, our place is mainly cities and large towns, which however are unwilling or unable to combine in its defence.

The effect of the county's internal divisions is reinforced by England's age-old metropolitanism, involving habits of deference, even submissiveness. All nations have to live with their own geography and a history that is partly determined by it. In the vastness of the USA, individual states, even those created in the relatively recent past, their boundaries drawn with rulers across featureless prairies, their populations no larger than Yorkshire's or Lancashire's, attract a fierce political commitment unknown to English counties or regions. In federal West Germany, the power of the ten states (plus West Berlin) ensures that no single city or area achieves anything like the position of cultural and economic domination enjoyed by England's south-east. For it is there that most English fortunes are made, of whatever kind, and there that most prominent Yorkshiremen have usually found themselves, in more ways than one. Hartley and Ingleby, in their 'Yorkshire Portraits' (Dent, 1961) confirm the point. The scores of worthies whose short biographies are there presented may have had their roots in the county, but their work was mostly accomplished elsewhere[3], usually in London. As a result the book is not, as one might have supposed, about Yorkshire, but a cross-section of the important people of England. It is to the capital, indeed, that they have gone, not only to become known, but even to meet. We have seen them doing so in the 17th Century, and the strength of the Society of Yorkshiremen in London in the 1930s confirms the point. Modern transport simply makes it easier. And now there is TV. We may even sense, in pessimistic moments, a gradual but accelerating process, a nation once the sum of its varied and valued parts giving way to one standardised by the mass media even as the land itself is shrunken by fast trains and motorways.

Such are the forces ranged against regionalism in England; and such the prospects for a political Yorkshire. The paradox is remarkable: a strong regional identity producing so little shared political aspiration in its own name. There is indeed no certainty that if regions were ever invited to apply for devolved powers, Yorkshire — or even 'the Yorkshires and Humberside' — would be among those applying.

Little wonder that the Editor of the Craven Herald, himself a dweller in West Craven, where the name of Yorkshire's old rival is too powerful to be shrugged off as merely administrative, should, on Yorkshire Day 1986, lob his playful appeal over the politicians' heads — to 'the Grand Young Duke of York': *After all your wedding was full of tradition, as is your family, so you will sympathise with us, we feel sure. Fight with us for Yorkshire and the Ridings,* and the letter/editorial was addressed in the name of *Your loyal subjects, Yorkshire folk all, no matter what side of the boundary they have been unceremoniously thrust.*

County of York. But there is still the place — the important one — whose boundaries are not administrative, subject of a thousand books, focus of trade and commerce, an organising base for knowledge and sport, for clubs and societies. The one that includes the Wolds, the Dales (even Upper Teesdale) and 100 miles of coast. The one that you 'come from'.

Buffeted for over a decade by others, the old concept has continued to resist, with mixed fortunes. Despite attempts to restrict it to 'the Yorkshires', it will not be so confined. In the North Riding it has fought back on its own ground against a familiar name, one of its own; in the east new titles and old coexist. In the west, where its people face a special difficulty, it must survive mainly in the heart. Elsewhere it has gone on the offensive, leaping the Humber (and indeed the Wash); and Lincolnshire has been caught celebrating Yorkshire Day. Deprived of its place on THE map, it appears on several, with variously overlapping areas, for health, electricity, water and the like.

Its real enemy is still muddle. The Lord Lieutenant of Humberside declined an invitation to attend the 1985 Yorkshire Day service with carefully chosen words. He was *certain that his attendance at such an event would be misinterpreted by those people in the area who wish to see the county abolished.* One of his flock, at least, would not see it like that: *Goole,* a young man told me, *is in Humberside for administration and in Yorkshire geographically.*

That was more like it. The fight for Yorkshire is not against local authorities as such. It is the struggle to maintain a distinction. Cleveland (south) and Humberside (north) are in Yorkshire just as surely as Orne (part) is in Normandy (and, on a grander scale, Turkey (part) in Europe). Our place can accommodate any number of administrative areas, either wholly or partly, whether they bear a Yorkshire name or not; and people need not fear to be both 'Humbersiders' (or 'Clevelanders') and Yorkshiremen — like many before 1974 — and even to wish their local authority well, whatever it is called.... until the next reorganisation.

Action. So what is to be done? A natural question, though this is a record of feeling, not a campaign. The chance to assimilate official geography to real places may come with the next reform of local government; but even then — such is the power of inertia — historic identities would only be restored (in the Times's phrase) if the case were made strongly enough — a challenge awaiting all interested bodies, from the City of Leeds to the North Riding action groups and the YRS.

Meanwhile there is, as it were, personal discipline — keeping things straight for oneself. On Map 2 the place that is in its second millenium is shown, unlike the fourteen-year-olds, in capitals, its boundaries unbroken. In thought, speech and the written/printed word it helps, as an antidote to the media, to use its name alone. Any compass points preceding it need not usually, in ordinary life, begin with a capital, except in the east if a point is being made. As we have seen, 'North' needs extra care, for 'North Yorkshire' actually protrudes below the Humber's latitude.

As for addresses, rather than incite civil disobedience, I simply state what happens. The Goole man was a purist. You did not even need 'Yorkshire' for your address, he said — *it would be like putting 'England'*. Some of us, however, are quite unable to write any other word than that (with the code) under a name like 'Guisborough' or 'Goole' — the hand would refuse to move even if the brain could give the order. The policeman has not called and the mail always arrives.

More generally, 'Yorkshire and North Humberside' must be rejected; and 'Yorkshire and Humberside', a hybrid mix of a political term with a non-political, should, mentally at least, be translated into wholly administrative ones — 'The Yorkshires and Humberside', for that is the area usually meant. Ordnance Survey itself provides no warrant for calling the three Yorkshires together, 'Yorkshire'. The only maps which do that are occasionally to be found on tea-towels.

But what could be expected of others? Could County local authorities be advised — by those having the temerity — to confine sponsorship of teams bearing their own names to the sphere which they control: the schools? Could publishers do something about maps? *The boundaries of the new local government areas shall be mered by Ordnance Survey* said the 1972 Act. It did not say that all maps should be administrative or that only local government areas were real. The notion that Yorkshire's main role in English life was ever administrative is absurd. People live in it, play for it, write about it, holiday in it. It might be thought to warrant its own cartography, complementing the other sort. Those who seek a living out of that broad concept, the County of York, through books, newspapers, monthlies, might occasionally show that its map is not defunct. (The heroic YCA, meanwhile, have to make their own).

Ideas like these are personal. A more public code might be helpful — devised and used by all those with an interest in seeing Yorkshire and local government co-exist separately, without today's confusion: academics, tourism promoters, journalists, publishers, sports officials, ordinary folk (not least from around the edges) and politicians.

Such scope for leadership and cooperation!

FOOTNOTES

[1] County Councils' written evidence to the Maud Commission 1968.

[2] Ten years later came evidence that the opportunity might not long be delayed — a Times report (15 March 1988) of the Government's intention to remove (or curtail) the power of the shire County Councils. But would even their abolition mark a return to the old geography? Not necessarily, as the persistence of West Yorks, Greater Manchester, Tyne & Wear etc. after 1986 shows.

[3]Politicians, of course, must gravitate to Westminster, and Captain Cook and Martin Frobisher could scarcely have won *their* kind of fame by staying at home, but the point applies to many others — from playwright Congreve and joiner Chippendale to the Sitwells, (all London) to Delius (Paris), W. H. Auden (U.S.A.), Barbara Hepworth and Ted Hughes (S.W. England), and so on.

[4]Again, a reference provided by Father Francis.

EPILOGUE

'..the Bill seeks unnecessarily to alter not only the local government pattern....but also the actual geographical pattern of England itself. Presumably the ancient geographical counties are to be removed from the map, and people are to be expected ...to accept entirely new geographical and sentimental affiliations which will be foreign and unacceptable. It would be a fatal error to deny the importance of....dealing with the character of the people, their geographical position...and traditional county areas. (Ted Leadbitter, MP for Hartlepool, in Standing Committee D, 30 November 1971[4]).

Prophetic words. What followed was 'cultural vandalism' (Colin Holt's verdict) of the first order. If only we had understood what was afoot, we 'romantics', or, having understood, known what to do.

As the years pass changes come rapidly, large and small, while adaptability is finite. For some the stumbling block is the decimal coinage and/or the measuring of waistlines in millimetres. Schools change, or are abolished. Then comes EEC membership, and all the while a social revolution proceeds, the Pill, drugs, Aids. And harder than these for many are cataclysmic upheavals on the economic scene — the collapse of staple industries — in Yorkshire and elsewhere — leading to the wretchedness of unemployment and demoralised communities. Here misery can simmer all the time and may boil to anger and violence.

The changes outlined here are not of this kind. The loss of your place — though its traditions and identity are yours — will not normally make men seethe all day long. *Telling people that they no longer lived where they thought they had lived all their lives* — the Yorkshire Post's charge against the Post Office — is literally shocking, but signers of petitions, voters in referenda, and even those who organise them, have more pressing things to think about, like jobs, if they have one — and especially if they have not — and families. So the Boundary Commission's response will not provoke riots in the streets of Guisborough. Dislocation, rather, is like other environmental things... bad architecture, polluted air. Its effect is insidious.

Holy Ground. And in any case, we are not all alike. Thousands are scarcely aware, and certainly do not care, that they live in Yorkshire. Others care in varying degrees but among these geography and history count for little. It is more a matter of their own identity: they know that they 'belong' — especially if they are among the 4 million living under a county name which includes the right word. But the County of York is not their concern. It is a big place, and we have not been taught to see it whole.

For others, again, every one of the 'Broad Acres' matters — the land of Wycliffe and Coverdale, Tillotson and Hickes, Sedgwick and Wilberforce, of the YCA and the County Cricket Club, and of all the Yorkshire Societies in this land and others. For them, wherever they themselves live, there is no Yorkshire without Beverley and 'Barlick', Middlesbrough, Sedbergh and Saddleworth. (Nor, incidentally, any England without Middlesex, Rutland and Westmorland). They do not acknowledge a 'Yorkshire' in which the City of York itself is only half a dozen miles from its edge, and a so-called North Yorkshire stretches to its south-eastern boundary. They hold their part of England among the enduring certainties of life. Its 'abolition', or the amputation of parts of it, or the restriction of its name — however 1974 may be interpreted — is not to be countenanced. Researchers can still use its boundaries; those writing about it do not need to explain; sportsmen representing it do not have to apologise.

If any find such attitudes incomprehensible let them imagine the cancellation or disfigurement of another concept, not much older than Yorkshire — England itself. And let them acknowledge that people's feeling for their country begins with their own part of it.

Life and Death. Those in authority know this. Indeed they count on it. If the nation is threatened by war, 'sentiment' or mere 'quibbling with names' becomes patriotism. East Yorkshire versus Humberside is one thing: England versus the foreigner quite another. In the 18th Century the Green Howards were ordered by George III to take the county name...1st York, North Riding Regiment...*which may at all times be useful for recruiting.* In 1914, when German ships bombarded Scarborough and Whitby, the appeal was not to the love of England: *Men of Yorkshire..enlist today...show the enemy that Yorkshire will exact full penalty for this cowardly slaughter!* And that same awful year, at Keighley, the same kind of cry rang out: *Yorkshire, with its broad acres, dense population and strapping sons, must not lag behind in this life and death struggle.* Such language tallied with the feelings of those who responded, and with the labels under which they fought in two World Wars: East Yorkshire Regiment; King's Own Yorkshire Light Infantry; York and Lancaster Regiment; East Yorkshire Yeomanry; Yorkshire Hussars; and so on through all the long roll of the county regiments of England.

If the bonds between people and place, strong, but only half-understood, are valid for war, they are just as valid for peace; and when, long after peace had come, men saw their place again at risk, not from a foreign power, but from that same Parliament which had enrolled them to fight many years before, they remembered: *I lost my father in the first war and he was in the 4th Somerset as were hundreds of others; I fought for my beloved county, East Yorkshire....*Such was the tone of many letters....and on local government, of all things!

Benediction. On Yorkshire Day 1985, the congregation in York Minster were bidden by the Canon-in-Residence to thank God for their county, its saints and martyrs, its good traditions and customs, and for its people who through many centuries had rendered good service to the nation. Yorkshire said the Dean in his address, still existed in spite of county boundary changes, and his hearers were there to prove it; and then came the final prayer: *We beseech thy blessing on this ancient county and all whose office and occupation do service to its inhabitants, that judgement may be established in the gates, and peace and plenteousness within the walls of it; by faith in thee and to thy sole praise. Amen.*

The East Yorkshire Regiment
– life and death.

Shrine in York Minster.